# book *of* faith
# Advent Reflections

## While We Wait

Tanya Ferdinandusz
Pam Fickenscher
Kevin Ruffcorn
Mike Sherer

BOOK OF FAITH ADVENT REFLECTIONS
While We Wait

For information on the Book of Faith initiative and Book of Faith resources, go to www.bookoffaith.org.

Book of Faith is an initiative of the
**Evangelical Lutheran Church in America**
God's work. Our hands.

Cover design: Running Design Group
Interior typesetting: PerfecType, Nashville, TN

Library of Congress Cataloging-in-Publication Data is available

The paper used in this publication meets the minimum requirements of American National Standard
for Information Sciences—Permanence of Paper for Printed Library Materials, ANSI Z329.48-1984.

Manufactured in the U.S.A.

24   23   22   21   20   3   4   5   6   7   8   9   10

# Contents

Introduction . . . . . . . . . . . . . . . . . . . . 4

How to Use This Book . . . . . . . . . . . . . . . . 6

Bible Study: First Sunday of Advent . . . . . . . . . . 8

Reflections Days 1-7 . . . . . . . . . . . . . . . . . 9

Bible Study: Second Sunday of Advent . . . . . . . . . 30

Reflections Days 8-14 . . . . . . . . . . . . . . . . 31

Bible Study: Third Sunday of Advent . . . . . . . . . . 52

Reflections Days 15-21 . . . . . . . . . . . . . . . . 53

Bible Study: Fourth Sunday of Advent . . . . . . . . . 74

Reflections Days 22-28 . . . . . . . . . . . . . . . . 75

# Introduction

For many of us, entering the season of Advent (whether we know when it begins or not), is like the start of a big race. We run to the shopping mall, we dash from one get-together to another, we zip off to another shopping mall, we scurry around the kitchen making cookies, and we make one last quick stop at the mall. The four weeks of Advent are sometimes the busiest weeks of the year, and in the middle of all this activity, we sometimes struggle to remember what's really at the "finish line"—a baby in a manger, Jesus, the Savior of the world.

The weeks prior to the first Christmas were filled with busy-ness, too. Mary and Joseph and others struggled—as all people do—to make it through each day. Imagine the tasks involved in traveling on foot with your family from one town to another to be counted in a census. This was a camping trip in which the people had to carry all that was needed—food, clothing, and shelter. Bear in mind also that one of the travelers was eight-plus months pregnant.

When we read the story of Jesus' birth in the Gospel of Luke, however, we hear the quiet, humble beginnings of a story that has affected the world in dramatic ways. Perhaps that's a clue for us—to live the Advent season in a humble, quiet peace, while reflecting on the real reason for the season.

Advent traditions developed long before the season was officially named and became part of the church year. For centuries, Christians have spent the weeks before Christmas preparing their hearts and minds for an important festival. This likely involved personal reflection, confession, and recognition of their need for forgiveness. At the same time, church leaders preached and taught about the importance of celebrating Jesus' birth and anticipating his return.

This book, by offering reflections and activities for every day in Advent, maintains the tradition of remembering Jesus' birth and looking forward to his return. The benefit of this book comes in part from the daily discipline of taking time out for a conversation with Scripture, with friends or family, and ultimately, with God. This discipline involves a few minutes a day and can be connected to things you already do—meals, walks, morning coffee. Make a decision at the start of the Advent season to set aside time for Advent reflections. That one choice creates a link with the first people of the story and millions since who have joined to celebrate the difference Jesus makes in this world.

In 2007 the Evangelical Lutheran Church in America (ELCA) affirmed the centrality of the Bible to Christian life and faith, and at the same time recognized the reality of biblical illiteracy in the church. This resulted in the ELCA's Book of Faith initiative, which invites us to open Scripture and join the conversation. By looking at the Bible through different lenses—historical, literary, Lutheran, and devotional—anyone can enter into a dialogue with God's Word in ways that lead to deeper understanding and spiritual growth.

As a Book of Faith resource, this book offers opportunities to open the Scriptures and join the conversation each day during Advent. The emphasis here is on the devotional lens, but the other lenses are used to provide insights into Scripture as well. The conversation can be shared with others through the questions provided, or it can go deeper in personal reflection. Daily activities offer hands-on experiences of the texts and what they mean for today.

Taking time for reflection during Advent can help us forget some of the busy-ness of the season, appreciate this time of waiting and watching, anticipate the second coming of Jesus, and find joy in God's presence every day. May your Advent reflections excite you and energize you to celebrate God's love come to earth that first Christmas morning.

# How to Use This Book

This book offers daily Advent reflections and activities, as well as Bible studies for each Sunday in the season. On the first Sunday of Advent, open the book to Day 1. (The season of Advent begins four Sundays before Christmas—the last Sunday in November or the first Sunday in December.) Keep the book in a prominent location where you'll have to see it—or perhaps move it—every day, so that it's easy to pick it up and read.

## Daily Reflections

This book contains three pages of reflections and activities for every day in Advent. The first page for each day is a reflection on a particular Bible text. Have a Bible handy to read the text first, and then use the reflection in the book to enter your own conversation with that Bible passage. The Questions to Ponder will help guide you through your devotional time.

### Faith Connection

The second page for the day offers you a thought-starter or a look at the Bible text through a historical, theological, Lutheran, or devotional lens. After reading the Faith Connection and the questions provided under the Journal Reflections heading, take some time to write in this book. Just let the words and thoughts or doodles flow. This is between you and God, so enjoy a quiet spiritual time. Don't worry about full sentences, grammar, or legibility. Write down things that are happening in your life, good and bad. List the things that are bothering you and let God give you the strength to take care of them. Allow the Spirit to work through you and enjoy a moment with God.

*The Work of Preparing*

The third page for the day provides options for using different parts of your brain and body to respond to Scripture and do some of the Advent work of preparing.

The first option listed for the day gives you ideas and suggestions for creating an Advent tablecloth over the course of the Advent season. If a tablecloth won't work for you, feel free to use other materials, such as a bed sheet, a very large sheet of paper, or placemats. (This is an activity for all ages. If you have younger children in your home, get them involved with drawing, coloring, painting, punching out shapes, gluing, choosing and placing stickers, and so on.)

The second option provided for the day has a more adult perspective. Generally, the activities listed here can be done on your own or with others.

The third option provides ideas for families to make sense of Scripture through hands-on activities that stimulate all the senses.

*Prayer for Today*

Each daily reflection ends with a prayer. In addition to the printed prayer, feel free to add your own. Open your heart to the Spirit's work during this season.

## Bible Studies

This book also provides a one-page Bible study for each of the four Sundays in Advent. Use the Bible study pages on your own or in a group to explore the Gospel texts for the Sundays in Advent. (Each study facilitates group conversation around three readings, which cover the Gospel texts for all three years of the lectionary.) If you are in a small group using the Bible studies in this book, take time for the daily Advent reflections during the week as well.

# First Sunday of Advent

## Be Watchful!

Matthew 24:36-44

Mark 13:24-37

Luke 21:25-36

Waiting . . . watching . . . reading the signs. These are the themes of the Gospel texts for the first Sunday of Advent. Today's texts are strong reminders to stay alert and watchful, living as though Jesus might return at any time.

1. Before you read the texts for today, list the expectations you have for this Advent season. What do you think may happen in the next four weeks? What events do you have planned? Are you looking forward to these days, or are you anxious?

2. Review each of the texts now. Notice the "signs" of the end mentioned in the texts. Draw or "doodle" what the world might look like according to these passages.

3. The first generations of Christians probably expected Jesus to return in their own lifetimes. How might living with this expectation change the way they read these texts? How do you think it might it have changed the way they lived?

4. Each new generation has waited and watched for Jesus to return. And still we are waiting for it to happen. Does this situation change the way you read these texts? If so, how?

5. When you think about the future, which words most often come to mind?

_____ gloom and doom          _____ peace and prosperity

_____ questions and mystery     _____ joy and wonder

_____ Other _____

6. What do you think of the following statement? What, if anything, does it have to do with "being watchful"?

   _Looking to the future is really about how we live in the present._

## Day 1: Sunday

## Who said Jesus will come again?

Acts 1:6-11

> *Key Verse:* They said, "Men of Galilee, why do you stand looking up toward heaven? This Jesus, who has been taken up from you into heaven, will come in the same way as you saw him go into heaven." Acts 1:11

All thoughtful parents teach their children not to enter into conversations with strangers, or even to listen to them. It's a safety issue. But sometimes it's the stranger who brings the good news we really need.

Our daughter once drove from Indiana to visit her sister, a student at Wartburg College. It was winter and she found herself caught in a classic Midwestern blizzard. Entering Waverly, Iowa, her car slid into a snowbank. She couldn't get out. She told us later that, as she puzzled over what to do, a stranger suddenly appeared at the driver's window of her car and told her to try again while he pushed. He got her back on the highway, but when she turned back to thank him, he was gone and there was no evidence of his having been there. The incident made her, and her parents, reflect on the possibility of angelic visitations, even in our day.

In today's reading, Jesus' dispirited followers are in a panic. They just watched their powerful best friend, with whom they'd only recently enjoyed an unexpected and amazing reunion, disappear. It doesn't seem like the right time to be encountering or listening to strangers. Yet a pair of them appear.

Their message? "He's coming back. It will be in a way as unexpected as his departure." Implied in their words is another message: "Don't stand around waiting. Remember what he taught you, and do something useful in the meantime."

Advent begins today. While we wait for the one we know and love to appear, let's keep our eyes and ears tuned to strangers in our midst. God has a way of using them, on our behalf, when we least expect it.

*Questions to Ponder*

- How do you visualize Jesus' location, as we continue to wait for his return?
- How do you think the disciples felt when angels appeared?

## Faith Connection

The Greek word *angelos* is best translated as "messenger." The Bible is full of stories about angel visits. One of the reasons their appearance is so unsettling is that their coming is unexpected, and their identities are unknown to us. The acid test for believers, however, is not whether we know the messenger, but whether the message is helpful and true.

*Journal Reflections*

- Have you ever received a message of hope from a person you didn't know? What did you experience?
- Has anyone ever told you that you were a messenger of hope to them when they really needed it? How are you a messenger of hope to others?

## The Work of Preparing

*Advent Tablecloth*

1.  Find a tablecloth you can write on (or use a very large sheet of paper) for the next four weeks. Keep it out, if possible, to remind you to complete each day's activities.
2.  Write "Advent" and the year on the tablecloth, and then sign your names.
3.  Optional: Use letter stickers to spell out your names and the word "Advent," and number stickers to show the year.

*Who Said This?*

1.  List some well-known sayings of famous people, including storybook characters, like "To be or not to be . . ." or "You can't lie! So tell me, puppet, . . . where . . . is . . . Shrek?"
2.  Devise a simple scoring system and conduct a "Who said this?" quiz. You can play this as a team game.
3.  Pose the question: "Who has said that Jesus will come again?" Search the Scriptures to find out (Matthew 24:30-31; Acts 1:9-11; 1 Thessalonians 4:14-17; 2 Thessalonians 2:1-2; 2 Peter 3:8-13).

*Sky Gazing*

1.  Go outdoors; if this is not possible, gather on a balcony or near a window. Have everyone sky gaze and name different things they see (or would usually see) in the sky (clouds, stars, sun, airplanes, birds).
2.  Challenge players to make a creative connection—even a vague one—between each object and some aspect of the story in today's reading (for example, airplanes rise from the ground into the air; Jesus was taken from earth to heaven).

## Prayer for Today

Loving God, you do not leave your faithful people without hope. Thank you for the promise of Jesus' return. Thank you for his life and ministry in our world. Thank you for speaking to us, even when the messengers who come seem strange and unsettling to us. We look forward to meeting Jesus. We pray in Advent hope. Amen.

## Day 2: Monday

### How will Jesus come again?

Luke 21:25-27

> 💬 *Key Verse:* Then they will see "the Son of Man coming in a cloud" with power and great glory. Luke 21:27

The late composer and director of the National Lutheran Choir, Larry Fleming, left the church a wonderful legacy with his arrangement of an old gospel song. "Give Me Jesus" soars with such energy and power, its performance almost seems to pierce heaven itself.

An appreciative audience member was deeply moved after hearing a Lutheran college choir sing this piece. She was especially captivated by the phrase, "And when I come to die, give me Jesus." Afterwards she told the conductor, "Now I'm no longer afraid to die."

As we anticipate Jesus' return, we have the promise of his love and embrace, sealed by our baptism. The description of the return of the Son of Man in Luke comes with a promise. The Son of Man will return with power and glory. This is an event for the end of the ages. Not many of us will experience it.

It's more likely that we'll meet Jesus at the end of our lives. Like the woman at the choir concert, we can say with confidence, "I'm not afraid to die." We can let go of things that ultimately don't matter, and say (in the words of the song), "You may have all the rest. Give me Jesus."

*Questions to Ponder*

- If you knew Jesus was returning for you tomorrow morning, would you change anything in your life between now and then? If so, what?
- To paraphrase a bumper sticker, "Jesus is coming back and he's really, really angry." What's helpful about that statement? What's not?

## Faith Connection

Early Christians were confident that the world would end soon. The apostle Paul demonstrates this conviction in his letters to young churches. It's possible this hope and belief enabled baptized believers to continue in the face of ridicule, rejection, and persecution.

Christians in North America generally do not face similar dire conditions today. If anything, we are tempted to sympathize with the message on a sign carried by a robed prophet pictured in a *New Yorker* magazine cartoon. The placard read, "Unfortunately the world is going to drag on." The truth is, God can and will surprise us, on a timetable not of our making.

*Journal Reflections*

- How does God's promise to return in glory help you to live as a disciple of Jesus?
- How can God's promise to return with power help you move forward, especially in situations you would like to see changed for the better?

## The Work of Preparing

### *Cloud on a Cloth*

1. Have the youngest person present draw a large cloud on your Advent tablecloth.
2. Invite the oldest person to write inside that cloud the words JESUS, POWER, and GLORY as a reminder of Jesus coming again.
3. Optional: Use letter stickers to spell out the words. Below the cloud, make a picture of Jesus coming in power and glory, or a picture of what you think God's glory looks like.

### *Cloud-Gazing*

1. Take time to cloud-gaze outdoors or near a window.
2. Let the clouds lead you to reflect on this: God's presence was made known among the Israelites in a pillar of cloud. Thick cloud covered Mt. Sinai when God gave the Ten Commandments. God spoke from a cloud when Jesus was transfigured or transformed before a small group of disciples. Jesus was taken up in a cloud at his ascension—and will return the same way.
3. Talk to the "Cloud-Creator" about how all this makes you feel.

### *Cloud Doodles*

1. Form pairs and give each pair a sheet of paper and coloring material.
2. Have each person take turns drawing a cloud with their eyes closed.
3. Next have pairs work together to turn their doodles into a picture that illustrates some part of today's key verse or today's Bible passage.
4. Admire your creations.

## Prayer for Today

Loving God, we long to see you at work in our midst. Help us to draw energy from your promise that our work in your name will be vindicated by your glorious return. Keep us from despair, trusting always in your promises. We pray in Advent hope. Amen.

## Day 3: Tuesday

## Why will Jesus come again?

Hebrews 9:23-28

🗨 *Key Verse:* So Christ, having been offered once to bear the sins of many, will appear a second time, not to deal with sin, but to save those who are eagerly waiting for him. Hebrews 9:28

A recently-converted Christian was eager to lead others, including some he considered to be "lukewarm" believers, into a vibrant faith like his. He asked a casual acquaintance, "Do you know the day and the hour you were saved?" His friend answered, "Yes. I know the day and the hour I was saved. It was a Friday, during Passover week in A.D. 30, outside the city gates of Jerusalem, around 3:00 in the afternoon."

We can be certain that, because of our baptism and the solid promise that undergirds it, our sins were forgiven and our destiny guaranteed even before we knew what was happening. We have the opportunity to grow into our baptism and behave like the saved people we already are.

When Jesus returns for us, it will be less like a final showdown and more like the last roundup. Why will Jesus return? To gather to himself those he has loved into the heavenly family.

We may like to speculate on what God will do with those who are not baptized or who have not lived as though they have been. In the end, it's God's task to determine this. It's our opportunity to live grace-fully, so that others aren't tempted to miss the great reunion.

*Questions to Ponder*

· Lutheran Christians don't stress personal conversion experiences, but rather thankful response to a gracious God. How does it help you to know this?
· Does believing that salvation is God's business let the faithful "off the hook" or make mission and outreach more urgent? Why do you think so?

## Faith Connection

In recent years a series of books described Jesus' sudden return and the terror it struck in the hearts of the unsaved. The story lines illustrated a belief held by some that God will "rapture" (snatch safely away) the believers and then annihilate everyone else. "Rapture theology" uses fear to drive those who are uncertain about their eternal destiny to Christ. Lutheran Christians focus instead on God's grace, which shows us that Jesus is not an angry avenger but rather a loving rescuer, one who draws forgiven sinners to himself.

*Journal Reflections*

· What things can you do to make your waiting for Jesus more meaningful?
· How has the assurance of salvation, which God provides you, shaped your faith walk this week?

## The Work of Preparing

### 📖 *Sin and Salvation*

1. Write SALVATION in large letters on your Advent tablecloth, using a different color for the letters S, I, N.

2. Read Matthew 1:21 aloud. Jesus came that first Christmas to save people from their sins. Draw attention to the letters in SIN. Jesus dealt with our sin by his death on the cross. When Jesus comes the second time, he will complete his work of redeeming all creation.

### 📖 *Advent Means Arrival*

1. Advent means arrival. When someone special is due to arrive, we make plans and preparations to welcome that person. During Advent, we not only look forward to Jesus' arrival as a tiny baby, we also look forward to his second arrival in glory. Think about how the second arrival will differ from the first by filling in the chart below.

| Jesus' First Arrival | Jesus' Second Arrival |
|---|---|
| Baby | King |
| Local | Universal |
| Helpless | _____ |
| Not recognized by many | _____ |
| Worshiped by a few | _____ |

### 📖 *Away in a Manger*

1. Gather near a nativity scene or picture (or, if possible, set up a crib) and sing "Away in a Manger."

2. A little girl was admiring a nativity scene. "But one thing bothers me," she told her grandmother. "Isn't baby Jesus ever going to grow up? He's exactly the same size he was last year!" What do you think Jesus was like as a child?

## Prayer for Today

Loving God, you have not abandoned us. In the midst of life's uncertainties, you give us assurance that we are loved, forgiven, and destined for everlasting life with you. Give us grace to live as Jesus would have us live, so that those beyond the shadow of the cross may also come to know your great salvation. We pray in Advent hope. Amen.

## Day 4: Wednesday

## When will Jesus come again?

Mark 13:35-37

> **Key Verse:** Keep awake—for you do not know when the master of the house will come, in the evening, or at midnight, or at cockcrow, or at dawn. Mark 13:35

Religious denominations have sometimes been organized around the idea that we can correctly predict the day and the hour of Jesus' return. All of these predictions have turned out to have been spectacularly wrong. Members of one group, convinced they knew the exact time of Jesus' second advent, put on white robes and went up on a hilltop to wait (they did it more than once, trying to get it right). When their best reading of certain obscure Bible texts failed to give them the answer they needed, they morphed into a movement content to say what the Gospel of Mark tells us: "You do not know when the master of the house will come."

A devout Lutheran woman once said, half-jokingly, "I don't know when Jesus will return, but I certainly hope it doesn't happen while I'm in the shower." That sounds amusing to us, but we shouldn't dismiss the thought. Jesus' return for most of us will be when our lives end. That can happen while we're sleeping, while we're struggling with a life-threatening disease, while we're driving on a four-lane highway, or while we're in the midst of a natural disaster.

How can we be prepared to meet Jesus when we know he could come at the least expected—and least convenient—time? The best answer may be the simplest one. We prepare for the unexpected before it arrives. Remembering the words of the apostle Paul might be the best preparation of all: "Whether we live or whether we die, we are the Lord's" (Romans 14:8).

*Questions to Ponder*

- Why do you think so many people are eager to know precisely when the world will end?
- What do you think of a God who keeps us in suspense about Jesus' return?

## Faith Connection

In some areas of life what you don't know can hurt you. If you don't know there's high voltage on the other side of the fence, you could be in big trouble opening (or climbing over) the gate. When it comes to the purposes of God, what we don't know can actually *help* us. If we don't know how, when, and where God plans to intervene in human experience, we are set free to live God-pleasing lives without watching the calendar or the clock. If we knew the day of our death, it might paralyze us. Not knowing can liberate us to embrace Martin Luther's directive in his Small Catechism to thank, praise, serve, and obey God from day to day.

*Journal Reflections*

- When in your recent experience have you found that ignorance is truly bliss? When isn't it?
- How have you learned to discipline yourself so that your lack of knowledge about God's timetable does not lead you into complacency or careless living?

## The Work of Preparing

🔖 *Clock on a Cloth*

1. Draw a clock face on your Advent tablecloth, but don't include the clock hands.
2. Read today's Key Verse aloud, and draw four giant question marks on the clock to show that we just don't know whether Jesus will come in the evening, at midnight, at cockcrow, or dawn.
3. Optional: Next to the clock, make a picture that shows morning, afternoon, evening, or all three.

🔖 *TIMES Challenge*

1. Have a stopwatch or timer available.
2. Make five-letter words using the letters T, I, M, E, and S. Set a time limit of two minutes or stop when someone manages to find all four words. (See answers at the bottom of this page.)

🔖 *What Time?*

1. Construct a simple paper-plate clock or use a toy clock.
2. Ask time-specific questions about activities relevant to family members (When do you leave for school? When does X get home from work?). As times are called out, younger family members move the clock hands to show that time.
3. Finally, ask: "What time will Jesus come again?" Keep moving the clock hands round and round as you conclude that we just don't know the dates or times for this.

## Prayer for Today

Loving God, we wonder what the future holds. In the midst of the terrors of daily life, through times both peaceful and stormy, we are often tempted to despair. You have promised that our lives are destined for a blessed ending, safe in your everlasting arms. Help us to live by faith, not by sight. We pray in Advent hope. Amen.

(Answers: items, mites, emits, smite)

## Day 5: Thursday

## Who really knows when Jesus will come again?

Matthew 24:36-44

> *Key Verse:* But about that day and hour no one knows, neither the angels of heaven, nor the Son, but only the Father. Matthew 24:36

We've all heard the expression. A public official is asked when a highway project will be completed. A frustrated parent is quizzed about the whereabouts of an errant teenager. A merchant is queried about when the high price of a commodity will come down again. The common answer: "God only knows." That expression is really an attempt to suggest, "Nobody really knows." Or, if anybody does know, it's God—but God isn't telling.

Jesus' message to us in Matthew 24:36-44 is striking. Concerning the return of the Son of Man, Jesus himself is in the dark. So are the angels, God's messengers. That seems amazing to us. Jesus is coming back, but he himself doesn't know when.

How long will the universe last? God only knows. Will it end as the book of Revelation suggests, or is that description an example of symbolic writing, not to be taken literally? God only knows. Will everyone be saved, or only those with pure theology or pure hearts? God only knows.

We can be content to leave the knowledge of last things to the mind of the Creator. Who can better serve as the custodian of such knowledge than the one who put it all together in the first place?

*Questions to Ponder*

- Does it surprise you that the Creator knows something that even the Son of God does not? Does this trouble you or comfort you? Why?
- How does the realization that our parents, mentors, and teachers don't know everything help us toward a more mature understanding of God?

## Faith Connection

There is an unsolved puzzle in Christian theology. Some catechisms (and theology books) affirm that God is "all knowing." But this creates a problem. If God knows everything that will happen before it occurs, what does that mean for our ability to choose between good and evil? One solution may be this: God has the ability to know, but God overlooks some things, for the sake of the human family. God reserves, however, the privilege of knowing and controlling the outcome—the ending—of all things. The truth about God's knowledge may be more complex than that, but this explanation may serve our purposes sufficiently, while we "see in a mirror, dimly" (1 Corinthians 13:12).

*Journal Reflections*

• What would you most like to do in service to God this week?
• How does knowing God was fully human, like you, help you on your daily walk?

## The Work of Preparing

*Questions*

1. Have each person think of a question that is important, which the Bible doesn't seem to answer.
2. Share your questions and have each person draw a big question mark in one corner of the Advent tablecloth.
3. Consider this—we may find answers to *some* of these questions, but to the question, "When will Jesus come again?" Jesus himself says that only God knows the answer.
4. Optional: Next to one of the question marks, make a picture of what you think God might look like.

*Preparing on Paper*

1. Find a way to look at a newspaper, magazine, or online news source.
2. Spend a few minutes looking for crime stories.
3. Share the stories and ask the following questions.
   - What, if anything, could have been done to prepare for or prevent these crimes?
   - Where is God in the middle of these crimes?
   - What difference does waiting for Jesus make in how we think about crime and its effects?

*Taken on Trust*

1. Distribute a simple snack.
2. When we accept a snack, we trust that we won't receive spoiled or poisonous food. We don't know *when* Jesus will return, but because of our faith in God, we don't have to know when—we can be content to trust that Jesus will come back, simply because he has said so.

## Prayer for Today

Loving God, we are astonished by the depth and the breadth of your trust in us. You have not made us puppets on strings, but have given us free reign to choose good or evil in your realm. Make us content to leave questions about life's end in your hands. Show us the way we should go in our daily walk, and keep us on your path until the end of life, when we will meet Jesus. We pray in Advent hope. Amen.

## Day 6: Friday

## What will it be like when Jesus comes again?

Daniel 7:13-14

> 💬 *Key Verse:* To him was given dominion and glory and kingship, that all peoples, nations, and languages should serve him. His dominion is an everlasting dominion that shall not pass away, and his kingship is one that shall never be destroyed. Daniel 7:14

A young boy listened attentively as his Sunday school teacher described the trial of Jesus, followed by his crucifixion. After retelling the story from the Gospel of Mark, the teacher asked, "How do you think Jesus' friends felt, watching these things happen?" It was all too much for the impressionable lad. He blurted out, "Jesus was their king! If I'd been there, I would have taken those awful people and beat the living daylights out of them!"

The response was unexpected, but not surprising. The boy had gotten into the story and was caught up in the injustice of it all. He wanted retribution, and a turning of the tables. His depth of feeling matched that of the people of God who watched foreigners wreck their temple in Jerusalem, and the first Christians who saw their enemies trample on their beliefs and persecute their leaders.

What does a godly person do when there seems to be no justice in the world? The writer of Daniel provided an answer that not only spoke to the Hebrew people in exile, but also to the first Christians struggling to be faithful against great odds. Daniel's message is dramatic: God will return and take charge. It will happen on God's timetable, but it will surely happen. We can count on it.

Since we know Jesus will return to rule in righteousness, why is it taking so long? God's calendar is not the same as ours. Advent is a good time to think about ways to open our lives to God's righteous rule. We need not wait for Jesus' return to start the process.

*Questions to Ponder*

- What might we do through our daily living to anticipate a world ruled by Jesus?
- What do you most hope will change when Jesus returns?

## Faith Connection

Christians need to read the Hebrew Scriptures (Old Testament) with humility. These texts have a different meaning for Judaism than they do for Jesus' followers. In its original context, Daniel 7:13-14 had a pre-Christian meaning. The one "like a son of man," coming with the clouds of heaven, was an unidentified future messianic rescuer. The Hebrews needed assurance that the covenant with God was still good, and that they had a future. For Christians, the same text resonates well with what we know and believe about Jesus and his promised return. It enriches our understanding of the Old Testament to be able to read this text on both levels.

*Journal Reflections*

- How can you learn and practice patience as you wait for Jesus' promised return?
- How does knowing that Jesus will return with power help to empower you in your faith walk?

## The Work of Preparing

*On the Map*
1. Sketch or trace a rough world map on your Advent tablecloth.
2. Write the names of some present rulers in the various countries. These are powerful people. But for how long do you think they will rule? Do we even know or remember who ruled in these countries 10 years ago? Sooner or later, these leaders' names will be taken off the map.
3. Write across your map, "Jesus is King forever. Jesus stays on the map forever."
4. Optional: Below the words about Jesus, draw a crown or make a picture of Jesus the King.

*Power Problems*
1. Skim through several newspapers, magazines, or online news sources and notice news reports that show power being misused (in the home, school, workplace, government organizations, and so on).
2. British historian Lord Acton said, "Power tends to corrupt, and absolute power corrupts absolutely." Discuss this statement.
3. In reality, no one has *absolute* power—except Jesus, and Jesus was sinless. How will you use the power given to you by God?

*Joy to the World*
1. Sing the first and last verses of the carol "Joy to the World" (with instruments, if you like).
2. Have one person read the words aloud, while the rest listen carefully.
3. Discuss these questions in relation to the carol.
   - What does the coming of Jesus bring to the world?
   - Why does Jesus create so many feelings of joy?
4. Sing the carol again, thinking about the meaning of the words.

## Prayer for Today

Loving God, we yearn to see things set right in our world. Where there is evil and injustice, we envision compassion and righteousness. Help us, as we await your coming rule of power in our midst, to do what we can in order to anticipate a just and healthy future through our actions here and now. We pray in Advent hope. Amen.

## Day 7: Saturday

## What should we do while waiting for Jesus to come again?

Luke 21:34-36

💬 *Key Verse:* Be alert at all times, praying that you may have the strength to escape all these things that will take place, and to stand before the Son of Man. Luke 21:36

Is it possible to be fully prepared for an impending time of trouble? The people of Iowa were warned, in early June 2008, that their rivers were about to overflow. They moved furniture and keepsakes to levels higher than previous floods had reached. As in previous floods, they built high dikes in low areas.

In 2008 the dikes were not high enough, and they were breached. Basements (and some living rooms) were filled with water. Areas never before flooded were inundated. Suddenly being prepared was not the issue. Finding the strength to deal with, and escape from, the calamity was.

Asked how they got through the crisis, residents and business owners reported that they drew on their inner resources of courage, stamina, and good will. Members of the communities indicated that they felt stronger after the experience.

Of special note during the crisis was the response of church people. In one town, where two neighboring congregations had historically harbored animosity toward one another, the divisions were forgotten. Those in the "high and dry" church opened their doors to those in the flooded church.

In some ways, waiting for Jesus' return is not unlike waiting for a natural disaster. We know it can come at any time, and that it can be devastating. We can't escape, and we can't avoid the chaos. But we can be prepared and resilient.

*Questions to Ponder*

- Why do you suppose Jesus' return will be dramatic and unsettling, instead of peaceful and non-disruptive?
- Where and how have you found strength to cope with times of trouble?

## Faith Connection

There is no assurance that the end of our lives will be without pain and confusion. We might hope that God will let us die quietly in our sleep. Unfortunately, for some the end comes with agony and great pain. Why should a benevolent God not grant us a peaceful death—especially if we have lived faithfully and well? The Lord's Prayer includes the petition, "save us from the time of trial." Some have preferred to pray, "save us *in* the time of trial." There is no promise that times of trial won't come. We have God's promise, however, that when they do we won't be left without hope.

*Journal Reflections*

- What helping individuals has God sent your way when you have faced times of difficulty?
- How have you found it possible to fortify yourself for the uncertainties sure to come in the days and years ahead?

## The Work of Preparing

📖 *Handprints*

1. Trace everyone's hands on your Advent tablecloth. If you are willing to try something messier, paint your hands (holding them palms-up) with washable paint, then press them on the tablecloth.

2. Across one of your handprints, write WORK; across another, write PRAY. (Or use letter stickers to spell out the words.)

📖 *Warnings*

1. Switch on the television news or skim through newspapers, magazines, or online news sources. Note any warnings given about climate or weather-related issues, diseases, war or civil unrest, etc.

2. Think about the kind of action that is usually taken in response to such warnings.

3. Jesus gives us a warning in today's Bible text. What action are we taking?

📖 *Work and Pray*

Form pairs and stand facing your partner as you chant this rhyme:

Jesus is coming (*at the same time, clap partner's right hand with your left hand and clap your partner's left hand with your right hand*)

Again one day (*clap partner's right hand with your right hand*)

While we wait (*clap partner's left hand with your left hand*)

We work (*clap your own hands*) and pray (*fold your hands as in prayer*)

(*Repeat same clapping pattern for the second verse below.*)

None of us knows

The time or day

But while we wait

Let's work and pray

## Prayer for Today

Loving God, we want to be ready and courageous at your sudden return. Give us strength and endurance, patience and resilience as we await an uncertain future. Keep our eyes focused on your promises and our feet on the path toward everlasting life. We pray in Advent hope. Amen.

## Second Sunday of Advent

### Watch for the Messiah!

Matthew 3:1-12

Mark 1:1-8

Luke 3:1-6

On the scene appears the prophetic preacher John the Baptist announcing the coming of God's salvation. John will preach repentance, but the one to come will bring the Holy Spirit, and in him "all flesh shall see the salvation of God" (Luke 3:6).

1. John the Baptist was sent to prepare the way for God's Messiah. Review the Gospel texts and list ways John carried out his task as "preparer."

2. John's message about the coming Messiah included quotes from the prophet Isaiah recorded over five centuries before John lived (see Isaiah 40:3-5; Matthew 3:3-4; Luke 3:3-6). List the things you think the people of Israel might have been hoping for in Messiah.

3. Have you ever heard these words from Isaiah and John the Baptist anywhere else? If so, where? What pictures come to mind when you hear these words?

4. You may have seen billboards, commercials, and even Christmas cards that state, "Just Believe." If our faith is going to be more than just "faith in faith," there needs to be an object of our faith. Read the texts for this week again and list the words and phrases that describe the one who is coming in the name of the Lord—the Messiah.

5. List ways that Jesus may have exceeded the expectations of people who waited for Messiah in his day. List ways he may have done or been something less than expected. Name some expectations you have of Jesus.

6. How can you prepare for the Messiah this Advent season? Identify a couple of ways and share them with others in your group.

## Day 8: Sunday

## Who is the Messiah?

Matthew 3:13-17

> 🔲 *Key Verse:* And a voice from heaven said, "This is my Son, the Beloved, with whom I am well pleased." Matthew 3:17

Baptism was commonly practiced by John the Baptist and his friends in the Essene community. The Essenes baptized themselves several times a day. For them, baptism was a way of keeping pure. It represented both cleansing from sin and beginning a new life. John called the people of Israel to this kind of baptism.

The *form* of baptism is not changed when Jesus approached John, but when Jesus steps out of the water the *meaning* of baptism is transformed. The heavens open. The Holy Spirit descends upon Jesus and fills him, and God speaks. "This is my son, the Beloved, with whom I am well pleased." This baptism identifies and commissions Jesus as the Messiah. His public ministry begins soon afterward.

Much more happens in baptism than sprinkling some water, administering oil, lighting a candle, and singing a baptismal hymn. Sin is forgiven and new life begins. And, there is even more! The heavens open, and the voice of God roars, "This is my child, my beloved, with whom I am well pleased." Claimed as God's child and empowered by the Spirit, the newly baptized (along with all the baptized) is sent out to tell the story of God's love and grace in words and actions.

*Questions to Ponder*

- If asked by a non-Christian friend or coworker why the Christian church baptizes, how would you respond?
- Think about your own or someone else's baptism. What is the most meaningful part of that baptism, for you? Why is it meaningful?

## Faith Connection

Baptism is more than a one-time happening. It's a watershed event that affects each day of a Christian's life. Certainly, Jesus "walked wet"—he carried with him the events of his baptism throughout the rest of his life. He was God's beloved son and filled with the Spirit. This shaped his ministry and enabled him to do what he did. Those who are baptized followers of Jesus are also called to "walk wet" in the reality of the water, the voice, and the Spirit in their daily lives.

*Journal Reflections*

- What does it mean to you to "walk wet," or to live in the reality of your baptism?
- What hindrances and obstacles prevent you from living in the reality of your baptism? What helps or inspires you to "walk wet"?

## The Work of Preparing

📖 *What Messiah Means*

1. *Messiah* means "The Anointed One." Christ is not another name for Jesus, or his last name. It's the Greek word for Messiah. Anointing involved pouring oil on a person's head. To be anointed was to be chosen and set apart by God for some special purpose. In the Old Testament, priests, and kings were anointed by God. (Read 1 Samuel 16 to see how King David was anointed.) Using different colors, write the following on your Advent tablecloth (or spell out with letter stickers):
Messiah = Christ = The Anointed One

2. Optional: Make a picture that reminds you of baptism or "walking wet."

📖 *What's in a Name?*

1. Find the names for Jesus that begin with the letters in MESSIAH. Here are clues: (M) 2 Peter 1:19; (E) Matthew 1:23; (S) Luke 2:11; (S) Luke 5:24; (I) John 8:58 (a little tricky); (A) Revelation 1:8; (H) Mark 1:24. (Answers are available at the bottom of this page.)

2. Reflect on what each of these names or titles means.

📖 *Sing to the Lord*

Sing this song (to the tune of "Mine Eyes Have Seen the Glory"):
Advent means arrival, it's the coming of the Lord
Advent means the coming of the Holy One of God
Welcome God's Anointed One, the promised Messiah
Let's sing alleluia!

Glory, glory, alleluia (*3 times*)
O come, Messiah

## Prayer for Today

Lord, thank you for sending Jesus, your beloved Son, to us. Thank you for also claiming us as your children and for filling us with your Holy Spirit. Give us comfort, assurance, and strength in our baptism, and help us to continue Jesus' ministry of sharing your love and grace in our words and actions. We pray in Advent hope. Amen.

Answers: Morning Star; Emmanuel; Savior; Son of Man; I AM; Alpha and Omega; Holy One of God.

## Day 9: Monday

## What does the Messiah show us?

Isaiah 40:4-5

> *Key Verse:* Then the glory of the Lord shall be revealed, and all people shall see it together, for the mouth of the Lord has spoken. Isaiah 40:5

People try to display success and glory in a number of ways, such as in the jewelry they wear, the clothes they dress in, the cars they drive, and the houses in which they live.

God's glory shines brighter than all of this. The psalmist says that creation declares God's glory (Psalm 19:1). Think about how the Hubble telescope pictures, a mountain sunset, or a walk in the woods during the fall can attest to this. God's glory is evident in the beauty of creation, and also in God's power and might, and in the abundance of God's gifts. Jesus the Messiah reveals God's glory to us most vividly. As he talks to his disciple Philip, Jesus states, "Whoever has seen me has seen the Father" (John 14:9). Jesus shows us God's power in the stilling of the storm, and the abundance of God's gifts in the feeding of the five thousand.

And yet, there's more. Jesus gathers children around him, showing God's concern for the smallest and the least. Jesus speaks to the woman at the well and heals several people of leprosy, revealing God's love of those who are powerless, judged, and excluded. Jesus dies on a cross, demonstrating the depths of God's overwhelming love for humankind.

Jesus the Messiah reveals God's glory, and so we praise God's power and might and the beauty of creation. We take comfort in God's love when we are judged or excluded. During the challenges and tragedies of life, we receive strength in God's grace. God's glorious love and grace comfort, strengthen, and empower us for life and mission.

*Questions to Ponder*

- What is your favorite story about Jesus, and what does it tell you about God?
- In what ways have you seen God's glory in your daily life, or caught a glimpse of it in the life of a friend, neighbor, or family member?

## Faith Connection

Those who have seen God's glory share God's glory. Because of this, the glory of God continues to be revealed today: A small congregation raises $12,500 for a family in the community with overwhelming medical bills. A person fighting cancer is surrounded by friends who provide transportation and sit with him while he endures chemotherapy. Houses are built through Habitat for Humanity. Clothes are given to an orphanage in Romania, and Sunday school students buy a heifer for a family in Indonesia. When others see these actions, they behold the glory of God's love and grace.

*Journal Reflections*

- How have you allowed the glory of God to shine through your words and actions?
- Pause for a moment and look at your family, friends, neighbors, and community. What needs do you see? What can be done to meet those needs and enable others to see God's glory?

## The Work of Preparing

*Glory of God*

1. Locate the words you added to your Advent tablecloth yesterday (Messiah = Christ = The Anointed One).
2. When the Messiah comes, God's glory will be seen. What kinds of pictures come to mind when you hear the word "glory"? Draw some of these on the tablecloth. Use bright colors, glitter, star stickers, and so on.

*Glory Story*

1. Find a nativity scene or picture that includes Jesus in the manger.
2. Reflect on the following questions.
   - Where do you see God's glory in the story of Jesus' birth?
   - Where do you see God's glory in the Easter story of God raising Jesus from the dead?
   - What are some ways to connect these two stories?

*Glory to God*

1. Sing Christmas carols (or other songs) which include the words "glory," "glories," or "gloria" (*O Holy Night, O Come All Ye Faithful, Angels We Have Heard on High, Hark the Herald Angels Sing, Silent Night, Joy to the World, While Shepherds Watched Their Flocks*).
2. If possible, have instruments available (even makeshift ones). Whenever you sing the words "glory," "glories," or "gloria," make an extra loud noise with your instruments.

## Prayer for Today

God, thank you for sending Jesus to show us your glory. We see your glory in the beauty of creation, in your power and might, and in your love and grace. Use us to touch the lives of others with your glory, so that they, in turn, may share your glory with those around them. We pray in Advent hope. Amen.

## Day 10: Tuesday

## What work does the Messiah do?

Isaiah 61:1-2

> *Key Verse:* The spirit of the Lord God is upon me, because the
> Lord has anointed me; he has sent me to bring good news to the
> oppressed, to bind up the brokenhearted, to proclaim liberty to the
> captives, and release to the prisoners. Isaiah 61:1

What is the job description of a Messiah? In biblical times people would have said, "A Messiah overthrows oppressors and establishes God's kingdom on earth."

People expected the Messiah to follow the ways of the world, where might makes right and the greatest treasures are comfort, security, and wealth. Several hundred years before Jesus walked the earth, however, the prophet Isaiah wrote that the Spirit of God would descend upon the Messiah and anoint him for ministry to the poor, captive, blind, and oppressed—all people in need. This certainly was a strange way to describe the Messiah's work.

Many people today would like to give Jesus the Messiah a different job description. How about a Messiah who gives us everything we want, who helps us become successful in the world's eyes? Or a Messiah who lets us be in control, instead of asking us to follow him? Or maybe a Messiah who is there when we need him, but otherwise stays out of our lives?

Jesus the Messiah doesn't do what is popular or superficial, however. He lived, died, and rose again to meet humankind's deepest needs. This does not merely improve our situation. It changes things forever.

*Journal Reflections*

- Can you see yourself in any of the groups listed by the prophet Isaiah? If so, how has the Messiah's work touched your life?
- What can the church do to share the good news of Jesus Christ with the oppressed, brokenhearted, captives, and prisoners?

## Faith Connection

In the *theology of the cross*, Martin Luther described how God is often at work in the most unexpected and unlikely ways. While we might expect God to be present in glory, power, and might, God is revealed in a helpless, newborn baby born in a manger. God's greatness is shown in giving up Jesus to die like a criminal on a cross.

*Journal Reflections*

- What kind of God or Messiah do you want or expect? What kind of God or Messiah do you need?
- Where in your life can you see God at work?

## The Work of Preparing

*Isaiah*

1. Draw a figure holding a large scroll on your Advent tablecloth.
2. Label the figure "Isaiah." Write the words GOOD NEWS on the scroll in large letters, or use letter stickers for the words.
3. Optional: Make a picture showing some good news you have received.

*What's News?*

1. Study the front-page headlines of several newspapers or check online news sources. What percentage of news reported would you say is good news? What percentage is bad news? (Some items may be neutral—neither good nor bad.)
2. Consider these questions.
   - What is the bad news the Bible tells us about?
   - What is the good news the Bible proclaims?

*Good News Game*

1. Gather four or more people, then find a space where you can move around and run.
2. Choose a "catcher" and a "deliverer." Everyone else must stand still. The deliverer "frees" people by tapping them and shouting, "Good news!" Those who have been set free can free others the same way. Anyone tapped by the catcher must stand still again.
3. When everyone is either captured or set free, begin a new game.

## Prayer for Today

Lord, we give you thanks and praise for sending Jesus to save us and to touch our lives in ways we didn't know were needed. Move in our lives in the ways you see as best. Empower us to proclaim your life-changing good news to the oppressed, brokenhearted, captives, and prisoners in today's world. We pray in Advent hope. Amen.

## Day 11: Wednesday

## How does Jesus claim to be the Messiah?

Luke 4:16-21

> *Key Verse:* The Spirit of the Lord is upon me, because he has anointed me to bring good news to the poor. He has sent me to proclaim release to the captives and recovery of sight to the blind, to let the oppressed go free. Luke 4:18

Imagine the scene. It is a Sabbath day, like any other Sabbath day in the town of Nazareth. The Jews gather at the synagogue, their place of worship. As usual, someone stands up to read from one of the sacred scrolls. This reading is from Isaiah, one of the prophets who delivered God's promise that one day a Messiah would come. But that was hundreds of years ago, and still the people are waiting for that day to arrive.

The man finishes the reading and sits down, but before the gathering can continue, he says, "Today this scripture has been fulfilled in your hearing." "Wait, what did he say?," people ask one another. The room buzzes with their comments. "Who does he think he is?" "He might as well have said he is the Messiah!" "Could he be?" "After all this time?" "Here in Nazareth? I don't think so!"

If you were there, what would you say and do?

Now move to today. Today is another day in Advent, another day when we might try to squeeze too many things into too little time. It may seem like just an ordinary day, but the Messiah is here! Jesus the Messiah has come, is coming, and will come again. God's promises are not forgotten. They are carried out, through Jesus, for us and the world.

*Questions to Ponder*

- While you wait during Advent, how will you remember that Jesus the Messiah has come?
- What difference does it make to you that God's promises are carried out?

## Faith Connection

Jesus comes to us as we are, with all our selfishness, faults, failures, hang-ups, doubts, and fears. He doesn't wait until we have totally turned our lives around (even if we could do that on our own). He doesn't wait until we've taken care of all the decorating, food, shopping, and gifts for Christmas. He is here with us right now, today.

*Journal Reflections*

- What do you usually do to prepare for Christmas? If none of these things got done this year, what would happen?
- Is it good news that Jesus is with you, as you are, today? Why or why not?

## The Work of Preparing

*Isaiah's Prophecy*

1. Locate the figure of Isaiah, which you added to your Advent tablecloth yesterday (Day 10). Alongside this figure, draw another figure holding a scroll.

2. Label the new figure "Jesus." On the scroll, write "Isaiah 61:1-2," or use letter and number stickers for this.

3. Optional: Next to Jesus, make a picture showing how you feel about the good news that Jesus is with you.

*Prophecy Fulfilled*

1. Find Isaiah 61:1-2 and Luke 4:18-19 in a Bible.

2. Start reading the Isaiah passage aloud, one phrase at a time. After each phrase, switch to the Luke text and find a phrase that echoes the same idea.

*Advent Scrolls*

1. In Jesus' time, the Scriptures were not available in book form, but on long scrolls (rolled up parchment or papyrus). Make your own mini-scrolls. Paste craft sticks at both ends of long, narrow pieces of paper.

2. Write Advent messages on your scrolls (a Scripture verse, line from a Christmas carol, or your own message). Decorate the scrolls.

3. Roll up your scrolls tightly from the bottom to the top. Exchange scrolls and read one another's messages.

## Prayer for Today

God of love, thank you for keeping your promises. During this season of waiting, remind us that Jesus is here with us now. Keep us focused on the gift of his presence with us each and every day. We pray in Advent hope. Amen.

## Day 12: Thursday

## What does a family tree have to do with the Messiah?

Matthew 1:1, 17

*Key Verse:* An account of the genealogy of Jesus the Messiah, the son of David, the son of Abraham. Matthew 1:1

Today it is popular to study genealogy. Knowing our ancestors' country of origin, travels, vocations, accomplishments, and even their failures, enables us to get a deeper sense of identity. We discover that we are more than a collection of genes, chromosomes, and social encounters. Rather, we are the latest act in a play that includes a cast of millions.

Jesus the Messiah was more than an itinerate Galilean preacher, or merely a footnote in Roman history books. Jesus was a part of a long line in Jewish history. He was a great-great-great-grandson of Abraham, father of the nation of Israel. As a descendant of King David, Jesus also continued David's dynasty. According to Matthew, Jesus was the latest of 42 generations of people with whom God had dealt.

Jesus' genealogy carries a powerful message. For Matthew's Jewish readers, Jesus' connection with Abraham means that Jesus is a relative. He fulfills God's promise to David that there would be a member of David's family on the throne of Israel forever. Jesus was also a sign of God's steadfast love through many generations that had gone before him.

When people saw Jesus, they remembered the stories of God touching the lives of people, generation after generation. They saw God's commitment to the chosen people, God's continued faithfulness, and God's overwhelming and continuous love.

*Questions to Ponder*

- Read through Matthew's genealogy of Jesus (1:1-17). What names stand out to you, and why?
- What would we *not* know about Jesus, God's Messiah, if we didn't have any of the information in his genealogy?

## Faith Connection

A family's history may be a source of pride, a source of embarrassment, a source of inspiration, or a seedbed for more questions. Whatever the case may be, our family's stories are our stories. In addition to our biological family, we belong to another family. We are members of the family of faith—a family with an illustrious heritage. Peter and Paul, Mary and Lydia, Augustine and Francis of Assisi, Calvin and Luther, Albert Schweitzer, Bishop Romero, and Mother Theresa are part of this family. These people are part of who we are, and their stories tell us about God's continued love and grace.

*Journal Reflections*

- What family stories make you proud or inspire you?
- Who are some of the people in the family of faith who inspire you, nurture your faith, or challenge you?

## The Work of Preparing

*Tree on a Tablecloth*

1.  Draw the outline of a Christmas tree on your Advent tablecloth.
2.  Draw a five-pointed star at the top of the tree and label the points "J," "E," "S," "U," and "S."
3.  Cut out or punch small circles from paper of different colors, and use glue to decorate the tree with them. (This activity could also be done with stickers, or the "ornaments" could be drawn on the tree.) Label some of the ornaments with names from Jesus' family tree (Matthew 1:1-17).

*Spiritual Family Tree*

1.  Who are the most prominent or significant people in your family tree? Why?
2.  Think of people who have helped you to be rooted and grow in faith. These may include people you don't know very well or even people you've never met (a pastor who influenced you or an author whose book impacted you). These people are part of your *spiritual* family tree. How are you becoming part of other people's spiritual family trees?

*Advent Tree*

1.  Plant a bare branch in a pot.
2.  Cut out or punch circles from construction paper or cardstock. (Use several different colors.) Attach string or paper clips for hangers.
3.  Each day until Christmas, take one of the circles, write down the name of someone who shares God's love with you (a relative, friend, or neighbor, for example), and hang the circle on the Advent Tree.

## Prayer for Today

Lord God, thank you for the steadfast love and overwhelming grace that you have displayed to countless generations. Thank you for the faithful people who have gone before us, who inspire us, and whose stories remind us of how you move in your people's lives. Thank you for making us members of your family through the cross of Christ. Help us to carry on the family tradition of glorifying you in our words and actions. We pray in Advent hope. Amen.

## Day 13: Friday

## What difference does it make that Jesus is the Messiah?

John 20:30-31

> *Key Verse:* But these are written so that you may come to believe that Jesus is the Messiah, the Son of God, and that through believing you may have life in his name. John 20:31

Where do we look for the Messiah? Some people have followed false messiahs like David Koresh and Jim Jones. Others have pursued wealth, excitement, adventure, or fame.

John has one purpose in writing his gospel. He wants to record the words and actions of Jesus so that people clearly see that Jesus is the true Messiah and place their faith in him. Who but the Messiah could turn dirty water into 60 gallons of fine wine, or feed over 5,000 people with five loaves of bread and two fish? Only God's Messiah could heal an official's son or cause a paralyzed beggar to walk. The wind and waves would only obey one sent by God. Only God's Messiah could be raised from—and conquer—death.

This is only a short list of the signs John records that point to the fact that Jesus is the true Messiah. John provides strong evidence in his Gospel that Jesus is who he says he is—God's Messiah. We might have a more comfortable life chasing after other things, but only Jesus promises to give us new life.

*Questions to Ponder*

- Besides the resurrection, what is the most convincing or meaningful sign to you that Jesus is God's Messiah?
- How would you respond if someone asked you why you believe that Jesus is the true Messiah?

## Faith Connection

The writer of John penned his gospel so that his readers would believe that Jesus is the true Messiah. The word John uses for "believe" is the same word that is translated "faith." It is a verb—an action word, and not a noun—a statement of belief. John's readers are invited to live out their lives in the reality that Jesus is the true Messiah. Luther wrote that our god (or messiah) is whatever we place our faith and trust in. All God's gifts are good, but they can't save. Only Jesus is the true Messiah.

*Journal Reflections*

- Jesus is the true Messiah. What difference does this make in your life?
- What other messiahs are you most tempted to place your faith and trust in? Why are they so appealing to you?

## The Work of Preparing

*Leading to Life*

1. On your Advent tablecloth, draw a signpost, pointing in the direction of the word MESSIAH (which you added to the tablecloth on Day 8).
2. Write the word LIFE on the signboard, or spell out the word with letter stickers.
3. Optional: Cut out the signpost from a separate piece of paper and glue it onto the tablecloth.

*Promises*

1. Flip through several television channels and watch some commercials, or skim through several newspaper or magazine advertisements. What do these advertisements promise? To what extent are the promises fulfilled?
2. Who or what is "advertised" in the Gospel of John? What promise is held out for those who believe that Jesus is the Messiah?

*Scrambled Signs*

1. Cut out large paper arrows. On each, write a need met by some object in your home—but scramble the letters. (See answers below.) Post the signs in appropriate places. Examples:
   Near bathroom or sink: LET CAT GONE
   Near a fan: FOOL COT EEL
   Near refrigerator: FIRY HUNG
2. Challenge everyone to unscramble the signs. John's Gospel includes signs that show Jesus is the Messiah.

## Prayer for Today

O Lord, we give you thanks and praise that through the life, death, and resurrection of Jesus we have received the forgiveness of sin, victory over death, and a new relationship with you. False messiahs tempt us away from Jesus and make us question whether Jesus is the Messiah. May your Spirit move in our lives and enable us to be faithful to Jesus the true Messiah. We pray in Advent hope. Amen.

Answers: TO GET CLEAN; TO FEEL COOL; IF HUNGRY.

## Day 14: Saturday

## How can we clear a path for the Messiah?

Mark 1:1-8

💬 *Key Verse:* People from the whole Judean countryside and all the people of Jerusalem were going out to [John], and were baptized by him in the river Jordan, confessing their sins. Mark 1:5

The Jewish religious system at the time of Jesus was corrupt. Money-changers in the temple precincts cheated worshipers. The priests grew fat off the sweat of the people. One religious group practiced strict obedience to the law. They blessed those who they believed pleased God and cursed those who they believed displeased God. Another group was in cahoots with the Roman government and offered a hollow faith.

At this point in time, John appears in the wilderness with a fresh, powerful, and life-changing message to people worn down by religion. He is blunt about the people's sinfulness, but he offers a baptism of repentance and forgiveness, and proclaims that the kingdom of God is near. Those who hear John see God in a different light.

Recent studies find that not everyone outside the church has rejected Jesus. Some of these people like Jesus, but they don't like the church. They see church people as judgmental and hypocritical, rather than as faithful witnesses to God's love and grace. Like those who first heard John's message, they may feel worn down by religion.

As individuals and congregations, we are called to make way for the Messiah today. We are called to repentance and forgiveness through baptism, so that others can see God's love and grace through us and the church.

*Questions to Ponder*

- Reread today's text, and imagine yourself traveling in the wilderness in order to hear John. What do you think it would be like to meet him?
- John preaches and then calls the people to respond by being baptized. How do you respond to God's word?

## Faith Connection

While we wait and watch during Advent, there is work to be done, too. Advent is a time to focus on preparing the way of the Lord. John the Baptist did this by announcing the coming of the kingdom and preaching a baptism of repentance and forgiveness. We continue this mission today by sharing the good news in relationships with people we encounter each day.

*Journal Reflections*

- Who has shared the good news of Jesus with you in your life? Who needs to hear the good news from you?
- How are you preparing the way for the Lord in your words and actions?

## The Work of Preparing

📖 *Paint a Path*

1. Starting from one corner of your Advent tablecloth, draw a path leading to the word MESSIAH (which you added to the tablecloth on Day 8). Be creative—your path doesn't have to be all one color or follow a straight line.

2. Along the path, draw three signboards and mark these CONFESS SIN, TURN AWAY FROM SIN, and TURN TO JESUS (or use letter stickers to spell out the words).

📖 *Turning From and Turning To*

1. Stand facing a mirror and imagine you are face-to-face with God.

2. Now think about sin. One way of thinking about sin is turning away from God. Turn away from the mirror and start walking away. Stop.

3. Repentance comes from a Greek word, *metanoia*, which means changing direction. Turn around. When you repent, you turn *away from* sin. But repentance is also *turning to God*. Start walking towards the mirror. Repentance brings us back into relationship with God.

📖 *Following Instructions*

1. On index cards, write different sets of instructions which will take someone from a predetermined starting point to a Bible or picture of Jesus (*face east, 10 paces forward, turn left, etc.*).

2. Give each person or pair a card and tell them to follow instructions.

3. Gather at the finishing point. If anyone has made mistakes, help retrace the steps.

4. What instructions did John the Baptist give to prepare people to meet Jesus?

## Prayer for Today

Lord, thank you for providing people who shared your good news with us. Thank you for giving us the gift of faith. Enable us to lovingly, creatively, and boldly share the good news with family, friends, neighbors, and coworkers. May you touch their lives as you have touched ours. We pray in Advent hope. Amen.

## The Third Sunday of Advent

### The Light Has Come!

Matthew 11:2-11

John 1:6-8, 19-28

Luke 3:7-18

The theme of watching continues on the Third Sunday of Advent, but we also move from prophecy to witness. The Messiah has come to bring sight and hearing and healing, and the poor will have good news brought to them (Matthew 11). And, along with John the Baptist, we are more than watchers now. We are called to be children of the light, living examples of God's mercy in the world.

1. Read the texts. Imagine that you are John the Baptist. How would you describe your role and your message to a reporter from the *Jerusalem Times* newspaper?

2. List all the places in the texts where you see evidence of witnessing or giving testimony. Name ways the texts "witness" to you.

3. Advent is a season of lights. How does the season add light to our lives? How do you see both John the Baptist and Jesus acting as lights? Sketch four candles on a piece of paper. Name each candle with one way you can be a light to others.

4. Jesus' arrival as God in human form created a new relationship between God and us. We can no longer claim a distant, observing God. Think of all the different places Jesus travels to help those in need. List the ways you may called to do the same. What, if anything, stands in your way?

5. Jesus, by example, demonstrated the personal way God interacts with each of us. The way Jesus offers forgiveness is a lesson to us all. How are you at forgiving others? What things might you do to forgive those closest to you during the holidays?

6. What one thing could you do to help someone—neighbor, coworker, stranger, friend, family member—better understand the reason for the season? (For example, identify someone who may be suffering from hardship, or invite someone who may be alone to share in your joyous celebration of the season.)

*Day 15: Sunday*

*Who is the true light?*

John 1:6-11

*Key Verse:* The true light, which enlightens everyone, was coming into the world. John 1:9

Sometimes, to tell a story, you have to start at the beginning. When the Gospel writers set out to tell Jesus' story, some started with the beginning of his ministry and others started with his birth, but John's Gospel goes back, wa-a-a-ay back, to the beginning. *The* beginning, when God created the heavens and the earth.

All of creation started with God's Word, including the first thing, *light.* John describes Jesus as that Word, that light, which was in the beginning with God, even before stars and planets and oceans existed. And God's generosity in making all things continues with this gift of sending Jesus, the true light, among us.

Light is a wonderful image for the presence of God, because we all know how necessary it is, and in this darkest season of the year we sense how important it is for any life to exist. Light is powerful, but it is not violent. It doesn't force its way in. We may say that light *defeats* the darkness, but we know that darkness isn't really doing anything. Light is something. Darkness is no-thing. Light only shines, and if you make room for it, if you reflect it, if you open a door and let it in, it changes everything.

So, John reminds us, God sends the true light, the light which has been around since the beginning of time and which cannot be quenched, no matter how long the nights get. Jesus, our true light, comes as God's pure and perfectly generous gift. His love does not force us to believe, it does not demand that we change. It only shines, and gives life where before there was nothing.

You could tell the story differently, but how wonderful to start at the *very* beginning, because God's eternal love has shone for that long.

*Questions to Ponder*

- When you tell the story of someone you love, where do you begin?
- When has God's love helped you see something in a new light?

## Faith Connection

John's Gospel is unlike the other three in many ways. While the other Gospels dwell on action, John is more interested in Jesus' words, and in finding the right words to describe who Jesus *is*. John's first chapter, often called the "Prologue," is a prime example of how John uses imagery and poetry to express who Jesus is. These images—light, Word, shepherd, bread, way—each give us a different angle on Jesus' unique identity. Each image gives us another picture of who Jesus is in relationship to God, and who Jesus is for us. But because each one is just an image, a picture, or a word, none of them fully captures the whole mystery. As fully God and fully human, Jesus is the mystery of God come among us.

*Journal Reflections*

- Where, in your life, do you need God's light to shine?
- How does it help to imagine God's generous gift of Jesus as something God intended from the beginning of time?

## The Work of Preparing

### Add Light

1.  In very large letters, outline the word "Light" on your Advent tablecloth. Draw the letter "i" in the form of a candle, with a candle-flame to represent the dot.
2.  Decorate these letters using colors that remind you of light. Add glitter to the candle's flame for extra sparkle, if you wish.

### True Light

1.  Reflect on this radio "dialogue" between a ship captain and an unidentified party out at sea:

    | | |
    |---|---|
    | Captain: | Change your course 20 degrees north. |
    | Reply: | Change your course 20 degrees south. |
    | Captain: | I am a Captain. Change your course 20 degrees north. |
    | Reply: | I am a Seaman. Change course 20 degrees south. |
    | Captain: | This is a battleship. Change course at once! |
    | Reply: | Change your course. This is a lighthouse! |

2.  Is Jesus your lighthouse—the one you who guides and directs you?

### Light the Candles

1.  Hang up several candle pictures (without flames).
2.  Form pairs and line them up at a designated "start line." Blindfold one person from each pair and give that person a crayon.
3.  The other partners from each pair remain at the start line and call out instructions to help their partners walk to a candle picture and correctly draw the flame. Amid the shouting, participants will have to listen carefully for their partners' voices.
4.  Many voices speak to us. Do we recognize and obey God's voice?

## Prayer for Today

Eternal Light, shine on us. Let your love fill us. Thank you for the gift of your life lived among us, full of grace and truth. Teach us to turn toward your light to give us life, and to reflect that light to others in how we live. We pray in Advent hope. Amen.

*Day 16: Monday*

## What are signs that the light has come?

Matthew 11:2-5

> *Key Verse:* The blind receive their sight, the lame walk, the lepers are cleansed, the deaf hear, the dead are raised, and the poor have good news brought to them. Matthew 11:5

"Are you the one?" We've all experienced that mix of doubt and hope as we meet someone. Maybe you interviewed people for an important position at your company, or decided about child care. Or maybe you remember that excited, fear-filled moment when you met the love of your life, and thought, "Is this the one?" The question is filled with hope, and a good dose of fear, because there's a lot to lose.

Hope and fear often go hand in hand. At this point in Matthew's Gospel, John the Baptist is sitting in prison and probably knows that his life is going to be snuffed out. He has crowds of followers, many who listen to him, but he is not "the one." But is Jesus? John longs to know that hope for Israel will not end with him. Is Jesus the one? Or has he misplaced his trust in some false hope?

Jesus' answer to John's disciples isn't about where Jesus comes from, his education, or pedigree. They can identify the Messiah by what they see. The good news is being *done*. Life is renewed. God's word of promise is made flesh in Jesus' life.

This doesn't mean that all the evil of the world has gone away. John is still executed, and Jesus' own life will soon be threatened. But in the meantime, despite all the hurt and oppression and poverty around him, Jesus offers good news, new life, in exactly the way the prophets predicted. Light shines in the darkness. The kingdom of God is at hand, and that is God's answer to all the fear, all the hope.

*Questions to Ponder*

- How do hope and fear get mixed together in your life? How do you trust when you are fearful?
- When have you seen or heard Jesus' presence in your life or in the world today?

## Faith Connection

"I'll know it when I see it," we sometimes say. But Jesus isn't just coming up with these "signs" of being the Messiah off the top of his head. His response to John's disciples is a reiteration of the prophets and the signs of God's presence scattered throughout the Old Testament. Matthew's Gospel often tells us in so many words: "this was to fulfill the Scriptures." In other places, the Gospel writer assumes that we will recognize when Jesus' story is fulfilling the words of the prophets and the longing of generations to see God's promise of salvation fulfilled. The New Testament never leaves the Old Testament behind. Jesus comes to fulfill the promises of old.

*Journal Reflections*

- Where do you look for evidence of God's presence in your life? Where do you think others might see it?
- If a friend asked why you think Jesus is "the one," how would you answer? How does your life reflect your answer to this question?

## The Work of Preparing

*Light and Hope for the World*

1. Talk about some things you are afraid of, then write the word FEAR in big letters on your Advent tablecloth.

2. Cut out large letters or use large letter stickers to spell out the words LIGHT and HOPE. Place these words right on top of the word FEAR on your tablecloth. Jesus is with us, and his light and hope help us with our fears.

*Give Us a Clue*

1. Form two teams. Give each team member, in turn, a light-related word (lantern, headlights, spotlight, lighthouse, starlight, candle, electric bulb) to mime for his or her team to guess. Devise a simple scoring system. In today's Bible reading, signs such as healing pointed to the coming of Jesus, the true Light.

*True or False?*

1. Prepare several questions which can be answered True or False (relating to Advent or based on the Bible passages for Days 1-16).

2. Give each person a flashlight (if you don't have enough flashlights, use cardboard circles with one side marked "T" and the other "F").

3. Form two teams and have each team stand side-by-side in a straight line. Teams use flashlights (or cardboard circles) to indicate their answer (*on for true, off for false*). The majority signal is taken as the team's answer!

## Prayer for Today

Holy God, shine your light in our lives, so that when we are blind, we may see. When we are sick, make us clean. When we cannot hear your voice, open our ears. Raise us to new life, and teach us to trust that you are the one in whom our lives rest. We pray in Advent hope. Amen.

## Day 17: Tuesday

## What is it like to live with the light of Christ?

Isaiah 9:2-3

*Key Verse:* The people who walked in darkness have seen a great light; those who lived in a land of deep darkness—on them light has shined. Isaiah 9:2

In Kate DiCamillo's novel *The Tale of Despereaux*, the tragic death of a queen has the power to plunge the entire kingdom into gloom. In the movie version, all the color drains out of the screen. The grieving king stops caring for his people and even his own family. The great feast of soup for which the kingdom is known is banned. It seems as if no good thing can overcome the sorrow that has descended on everything and everyone.

Only at the very end, when one act of forgiveness leads to another, and then another, do the skies clear. The sunlight spreads until finally it is reflected into the deepest dungeon. The light changes everything, even in that darkest place, just as forgiveness begins to change everything in the relationships between the princess, her father, and the people.

The people of Israel had seen many times in their history when it seemed that no good thing could emerge. One conquering empire after another had marched through, and all their prayers for freedom seemed to go unheeded. But again and again, light would shine on their path—just enough light to let them walk forward with trust that God had not abandoned them.

The light of Jesus shines into our lives that way as well. Sometimes it's just a small light in the night—a single act of forgiveness, a little bit of bread on Sunday morning. But that light, when it is reflected, when it is magnified by the church gathering together to proclaim God's promise in Jesus, has the power to change everything.

*Questions to Ponder*

- When have you seen a relationship changed because truth and light were able to shine into it?
- How have you seen the light of love or forgiveness spread from one person to another?

## Faith Connection

In *Beyond Words*, Frederick Buechner writes, "To repent is to come to your senses. It is not so much something you do as something that happens. True repentance spends less time looking at the past and saying, 'I'm sorry,' than to the future and saying, 'Wow!'" (HarperSanFrancisco, 2004, p. 343). As the prophets knew, in times of trouble, fear, and anger, only God's light can bring about real change. When that happens, however, we don't need to dwell on making sure everyone understands our sorrow. More importantly, we celebrate a grace-filled future by turning to a new life that inspires others.

*Journal Reflections*

- What does a dark place in your life look like? How does the light of Christ change that place?
- What place in the world cries out for God's light today? How can you help provide that light?

## The Work of Preparing

*People of the Light*

1. Locate the word "Light" that you added to your Advent tablecloth on Day 15.
2. Invite each person to draw himself or herself looking up towards the word "Light." (Stick figures are fine. Another option is to paste photos of yourselves beneath the word "Light.")

*Glowing in the dark*

1. Gather in a room that can be completely dark.
2. Set a timer for one minute (or plan to count to sixty).
3. Reread Isaiah 9:2, then turn off the light for one minute. In that time, think of ways that God's light can shine through you.

*In the dark*

1. Get a large cloth bag and place several objects inside it. (You might include a plastic jug, checkbook, sponge, baby's bottle, pencil sharpener, eraser, etc.) Tie the bag shut.
2. Play some music while passing the bag among each other. When the music stops, the person holding the bag closes her eyes, picks an object from the bag, and tries to guess what it is. If she fails, those who can see the object may offer hints.

## Prayer for Today

God, you shine your light into our lives through baptism, through faith communities, and through . . . *name people who are light to you*. We pray for shadowy places in our world where your light and your truth are badly needed. Give hope to those who are in despair. Teach us to reflect your light today, passing it on to every place we go. We pray in Advent hope. Amen.

## Day 18: Wednesday

### How is it possible for us to be children of God or children of the light?

John 1:12-13

> 🔖 *Key Verse:* To all who received him, who believed in his name, he gave power to become children of God. John 1:12

It is not unusual at some point in adolescence to look at our parents and wonder, "How did I get stuck with *these* people?" The Harry Potter novels are among the latest of many stories featuring orphans and foundlings who are raised with one set of adults but *know* that they really belong somewhere, or to someone, else. Teenagers keep their distance as they gain independence, struggling to gain their own identity instead of simply being "so-and-so's child."

We don't choose our parents, but what can seem like a burden as a teenager can also be a blessing. We all enter the world without a choice in this matter, and in need of people to take care of our needs and claim us as their own. Being someone's child means we belong. We will always be part of a family, no matter what.

In Jesus' day, the emperor claimed to be a "son of God." Being God's child implied royalty or special status that the whole world should recognize. But when Jesus, God's true Son, enters the world, he turns the tables by sharing his royal status with us. God adopts all of us—male or female, rich or poor, Jew or Gentile—into God's family. We do not choose. God chooses us (John 15:16). And no one can snatch us out of God's hands (John 10:28). Thanks be to God!

*Questions to Ponder*

- What does it mean that Jesus shares his "royal status" with you?
- When have you felt orphaned or like you didn't fit in with your family? What does it mean in these situations to be God's child?

## Faith Connection

John's Gospel begins with a "Prologue" that is more poetry than storytelling. Like poetry, it has a particular structure that leads you into the heart of the matter. Some literary scholars see in John 1 a "chiasm," a kind of "zooming into focus" that centers on John 1:12: "He gave power to become children of God." All the forethought of God, from the very beginning of creation, zooms into this moment—our adoption into God's family through faith in Christ. The center of John's Gospel is not just that Jesus is the Son of God, but that we who are called through faith become God's children. From the beginning of time God intended to welcome you into God's family.

*Journal Reflections*

- What are your joys and fears about being chosen?
- How does it feel to be chosen by God?

## The Work of Preparing

*Children of Light*

1. Find your names on the Advent tablecloth. (If someone did not sign on Day 1, take time for that now.)
2. By faith, we are children of God, children of the light. To symbolize this, decorate around your names using colors, shapes, or stickers that suggest light.

*Happy Birthday*

1. Consider the details of your birth (where, when, how much you weighed, your parents' names, etc.)
2. Reflect on how you became part of God's family.
3. Light candles (and sing "Happy Birthday," if you wish) to celebrate your birth by faith into God's family.

*Family Campfire*

1. Sit in a circle around a "campfire" (several lighted candles or flashlights). Please note that burning candles should not be left unattended.
2. Sing songs about light and about being part of God's family ("Shine, Jesus, Shine," "Light of the World," "Jesus Wants Me for a Sunbeam," "This Little Light of Mine," "Pass It On").

## Prayer for Today

Loving God, help us each day to remember that we have been chosen by you. Teach us to live as your beloved children, and to trust that there is nothing that can snatch us out of your hands. We pray in Advent hope. Amen.

## Day 19: Thursday

## What does it mean to walk in the light?

1 John 1:5-7

*Key Verse:* If we walk in the light as he himself is in the light, we have fellowship with one another, and the blood of Jesus his Son cleanses us from all sin. 1 John 1:7

At summer camps, some of the most important things happen around evening campfires. After a long day of playing, working, and sometimes arguing with one another, campers and their counselors find some mutual calm and appreciation in the glow of the firelight. In this light, people reveal who they really are and express appreciation for each other, for nature, and for God.

The harsh light of the afternoon, however, can have the opposite effect. We see each other's faults all too well. Our agendas compete with one another, and everybody grows tired of each other. Siblings cannot get along, and no one wants to set the dinner table.

The light 1 John refers to is something else altogether. The light Jesus brings is not like the warm fuzzy glow of fires or candles, or the harsh afternoon sun. It is a light that reveals the truth about us—that we are all God's children. It enables us to see ourselves and others in the light of what Jesus has done for us.

*Questions to Ponder*

- What helps you to see others in the light of God's love?
- What parts of yourself do you fear bringing into the light?

## Faith Connection

We don't know exactly who wrote what we call 1, 2, and 3 John. The author may have also written the Gospel of John. Most scholars agree that the writer of these letters and John's Gospel must have at least come from the same community, or group of communities. These letters and the Gospel of John use similar language to talk about Jesus and explain this amazing gift of God's presence in the Word made flesh.

*Journal Reflections*

- What does God's light reveal about you? What do you see that you might be afraid others will see?
- With Jesus as your partner, standing before God, how do the same truths you wrote about above look in light of Jesus' life and death?

## The Work of Preparing

*Fellowship Circle*

1. Locate the word "Light" that you added to your Advent tablecloth on Day 15 and the figures you drew on Day 17.
2. Take a thick marker and draw a circle or outline around the figures *and* the word "Light." This circle (or outline) reminds us that we have fellowship with Jesus the Light and with one another.
3. Add color, pictures, or stickers around the circle (or outline) if you wish.

*Let the Light Shine*

1. Put up a string of Christmas lights somewhere in your home. If Christmas lights are already up, turn them on and turn off all other lights.
2. While music plays softly in the background, think about one or two key phrases from 1 John 1:5-7 ("God is light," "walk in the light"). Ask God for peace and calm in your life this week.

*Treasure Hunt*

1. Obtain flashlights and small pieces of red, yellow, green, and blue cellophane.
2. Choose a "treasure hunter," who will remain in one room while everyone else hides the treasure.
3. No one is allowed to speak. Help the "treasure hunter" find the treasure with light signals (red—turn right, yellow—turn left, green—go straight, blue—go back).

## Prayer for Today

God of light, you shine the light of your truth on us, and sometimes the truth hurts. But your light also reveals us to one another, and helps us see how you love all your children with forgiving grace. Help us walk in that light every day, so that we have courage to face the truth and grace to see others as our brothers and sisters. We pray in Advent hope. Amen.

## Day 20: Friday

## What promise do we have from Jesus, the light of the world?

John 8:12-16

> *Key Verse:* Jesus spoke to them, saying, "I am the light of the world. Whoever follows me will never walk in darkness but will have the light of life." John 8:12

When we "walk in darkness," it isn't just the lack of light that's the problem. We're half-awake, stumbling about, or maybe there's clutter on the floor. It's the unexpected that's the problem.

Sometimes in the life of faith we try to help one another by describing our personal journeys. We imagine that our friends or family might have exactly the same path. If only we could let them know ahead of time what to look out for, we think, we might spare them a lot of pain. Wouldn't it be great if our sons or daughters might learn from us and not have all those unpleasant surprises on the way?

Most of the time life doesn't work like that. What I experience in prayer might be quite different from the person next to me. The path that led me through grief or a time of feeling spiritually lost might not be available to someone else. Sometimes the only way to follow Jesus is just to take one step, and then another. The light available to us might be just enough for today.

When Jesus says, "follow me," he isn't saying that the path will be predictable. The life of discipleship involves times of unexpected obstacles and unpredictable sorrows. If we knew exactly what the path looked like, there would be no need to follow. We could just go out on our own and make our way by ourselves.

Jesus doesn't call us to be spiritual lone rangers. He invites us to follow—so closely that we can hear his footsteps. He promises that there is no place he has not already visited, no obstacle in our way that he has not also encountered. He will shine just enough light of his love and forgiveness so that we can walk with security.

*Questions to Ponder*

- What does "just enough light" of Jesus' love mean for you?
- What benefit is Jesus' light if there are still obstacles?

## Faith Connection

In John's Gospel, the word "world" is usually a negative term used when John is describing how Jesus' message and ministry were not received by those around him. The light Jesus brings is always in contrast to the darkness of the world. Too many people would rather go on living without the truth than face up to what God's light reveals. The Pharisees based their authority on written law and teaching about how to follow the Torah, while Jesus bases his authority in something less visible, his relationship to the Father. Like the Pharisees, we cannot understand Jesus' light apart from this relationship to God. This is a kind of light that we only see through faith.

*Journal Reflections*

- How have you seen Jesus' light in times when you have encountered unexpected obstacles?
- What does it mean to trust in a relationship with Jesus instead of in facts, knowledge, and educated predictions about the future?

## The Work of Preparing

### Light of the World

1. Locate your world map on the Advent tablecloth from Day 6 (or draw a globe to represent the world).
2. Across the map (or around the globe), write JESUS IS THE LIGHT OF OUR WORLD or use letters stickers to spell out some or all of these words.
3. Optional: Around the words just added, make pictures and use colors or stickers that remind you of Jesus and light.

### Promise of Light

1. If you have a Bible, look up John 8:12 and underline the words.
2. On a piece of paper, use the words from this verse to make as many new sentences as possible. Be creative, funny, serious, or whatever strikes you. Have fun.

### Let there be Light

1. Give each person a flashlight or candle.
2. Say, "Let there be light." Everyone should switch on the flashlights (light the candles).
3. Say, "Let there be dark." Participants may turn off the flashlights (blow out the candles).
4. Discuss: Which is stronger or more powerful, the light or the darkness? (Even a dim flashlight or tiny candle flame can take away some of the darkness, but darkness can't take away any light. Darkness is not something in its own right; it's simply the *absence* of light.)

## Prayer for Today

Dear Jesus, thank you for offering your light to the world, even when people rebel against it. Help us to trust that your light is enough for today, even when we cannot see very far ahead on the path we're on. We pray in Advent hope. Amen.

*Day 21: Saturday*

*What are children of the light called to do?*

Luke 3:7-14

💬 *Key Verse:* Whoever has two coats must share with anyone who has none; and whoever has food must do likewise. Luke 3:11

In the 1982 movie *A Year of Living Dangerously* (Warner Home Video), eccentric photographer Billy Kwan goes about the poverty-stricken streets of Jakarta, Indonesia with more than a good story in mind. Billy records the suffering he sees among the families living in the shadows, sending home his reports to foreign newspapers. He continues to be haunted by what he has seen, however, sometimes writing long into the night with the question that John the Baptist's followers asked of him, "What then should we do?"

For Billy, the answer is twofold. First, he shines a light, recording the truth about the suffering he sees in the shadows of an oppressive regime. Like John the Baptist crying out in the wilderness, he uses prophetic words and images to move the hearts of the powerful.

At the same time, Billy finds one family to assist and brings them bags of rice and other basic necessities. These acts of compassion keep him connected with people who might otherwise just be characters in a story.

Poverty, violence, and all manner of sin bring suffering to human lives and can cause us to question the power of Christ's light. We might agree sometimes with John the Baptist's assessment that "the ax is lying at the root of the trees."

John's answer to the question, "What then should we do?" is simple and radical—give. If you have two coats, give one away. If you have more food than you need, give to those who have none. Doing these things lets the light Christ sends into our lives spill over into the lives of others.

*Questions to Ponder*

- What shadows of the world—poverty, violence, discrimination—most move your heart?
- Name one thing you have in excess. How can you give it away to those who are in need?

## Faith Connection

Some scholars think that John the Baptist's work in chapter 3 was originally the beginning of Luke's Gospel. Only in a later draft did Luke decide to go back to the story of Jesus' origins. One can imagine the whole story starting here, not as a story of Jesus' life but as the story of God's message to a people who were walking in darkness. John preaches the law—the hard news that God's people had turned away from God's purposes—and by his baptism of repentance prepares the crowds to hear Jesus' good news that the kingdom of God is at hand.

*Journal Reflections*

- How do you feel about being *commanded* by God to do something for your neighbor?
- How do you feel when you give to others from your excess?

## The Work of Preparing

*Light in the World*

1. Locate your name on the Advent tablecloth from Day 1 (and decorated on Day 18).
2. Talk about ways in which we can be children of light in our world (see today's Bible passage for some examples). Beneath your name, write or draw one thing you will do as a child of the light during this coming week.

*Reflection on Reflecting Light*

1. Reflect, for a moment, on the sun and the moon. The sun generates its own light. But the moon merely reflects the light from the sun.
2. Jesus says, "I am the light of the world" (John 8:12). But he also tells his followers, "You are the light of the world" (Matthew 5:14). How can we reflect the light of Jesus in our world?

*Reflect-the-Light Relay*

1. Form two teams, and give each team a flashlight and a mirror.
2. Mark two small spots on a wall. Designate a line beyond which teams cannot move.
3. The objective of the game is to manipulate the flashlight and mirror so that light is reflected off the mirror onto the spot on the wall.
4. Play this game relay-style, with each team member in turn reflecting the light onto the wall. Whichever team finishes first, wins.

## Prayer for Today

Jesus, send your light into our hearts and lives. Help us see the small acts of giving we can do for others. Show us where we have more than enough, so that we might share. Help us release those things we do not need so that we can be ready to receive the things we do. We pray in Advent hope. Amen.

## The Fourth Sunday of Advent

### God Is With Us!

Matthew 1:18-25

Luke 1:26-38

Luke 1:39-45, (46-55)

The day of great celebration is near, the day when we remember with joy that God did choose to come to us in the flesh, as a human child. His very name, Emmanuel ("God is with us"), defines this miraculous promise. Through a humble young woman, God's own Son would be born as a Savior for all the world.

1. Read the texts and let the amazing words sink in. What words or phrases touch you, or stir you, or make you wonder? Why?

2. In what ways do you see the faith of Mary and the openness of Joseph as examples of true servanthood?

3. Mary's song of praise (the Magnificat) in Luke 1:46-55 captures the essence of Christ's ministry to come. Describe what this ministry will look like. What questions does this picture of Jesus' ministry raise in your mind?

4. Reflect for a few moments on this statement: "Advent is not just about 'waiting' for something to happen; it's about making things happen in the name of God and for the sake of the world." How might this be true? What does the promise of Emmanuel ("God is with us") fit with this statement?

5. Go back to the original expectations you listed for this Advent season. Have those expectations been met? Did you let go of some of them as priorities changed? What have been the high points of the season? If you could do it over, what would you change?

6. As you reflect back on the conversations about the Bible texts for Advent, name one or two important discoveries or insights you had. How can these new insights impact the way you live?

## Day 22: Sunday

## How does Jesus bring about both justice and mercy?

Luke 1:46-55

*Key Verse:* He has brought down the powerful from their thrones, and lifted up the lowly. Luke 1:52

People who live in palaces sometimes feel uncomfortable. They know their luxury is made possible only by the sacrifice and suffering of those living in ordinary, or even impoverished, circumstances. During the Second World War, when Germany was bombing London, the working-class section of the city known as the East End took a lot of strafing and destruction. In a later air raid, Buckingham Palace was hit. The Queen Mother told the press, "I'm glad it happened. Now we know how the East Enders feel." Perhaps. But she continued to live in the palace, and the East Enders continued living a marginal existence.

When God invaded our world in human form, there were plenty of respectable venues available. Why wasn't the King of the Universe born in a king's house? In the world into which Jesus was born, the wealthy controlled nearly everything. Compassion toward the less fortunate was often in short supply.

Mary came from a low-class family. She celebrated her pregnancy with hopeful words, looking forward to a time when lowly people will be lifted up and privileged individuals brought low. God's concern is for those in need of mercy and justice. They are generally not found living in palaces.

*Questions to Ponder*

- What's your reaction to the idea that living with more than you need is stealing from the poorest people?
- How far from your front door do you need to travel in order to find someone crying for mercy and justice?

## Faith Connection

Reversal is a common theme in the Gospel of Luke. Jesus' teaching in this Gospel strongly suggests the tables will be turned. People of privilege will be forced to surrender it. People of no influence will be enfranchised. Understandably, this theme is not popular with those who believe they have a lot to lose. Many Lutherans immigrated to North America, bringing few possessions with them. Upon arrival, they often joined the ranks of the poorest classes. Generations later, many North American Lutherans are among the most prosperous people on the continent. Luke's call for justice and mercy might strike today's Lutheran church differently than it did generations and centuries ago, but God's concern for justice and mercy remains the same.

*Journal Reflections*

- When you believe you are being treated unjustly, where do you go for help?
- How did you feel the last time you showed mercy to someone in need of it?

## The Work of Preparing

*Star of Christmas*

1. Draw a large six-pointed star on your Advent tablecloth as a reminder that Jesus is the star of the Christmas story. Then draw smaller stars or put small star stickers on the tablecloth (as many as you want).
2. Optional: In each point of the star, write words that describe God (see Luke 1:46-55 for help).

*Merciful Judge*

1. A judge was hearing a case. The prisoner was guilty—but he was also an old friend. What would the judge do? "Guilty!" said the judge. The man could not pay the fine, so he was taken to prison. The judge left the courtroom, went to the prison, and paid the fine—the man was set free. On the cross, Jesus paid the penalty for the sin of the world. By the cross, Jesus also extends the gift of mercy to the world. What can you do to offer mercy to someone today?

*Magnify God*

1. Today's Bible passage is part of a song Mary sang shortly after the angel Gabriel's visit. It is called "The Magnificat" (from a Latin word meaning "magnify"). Mary "magnifies" God by singing about what God has done or will do. Read the Bible passage aloud and see if you can count how many times Mary says "God," other names for God, or refers to God using the words "he" or "his."
2. Make up your own song praising God. Add instruments (makeshift ones will do)!

## Prayer for Today

Loving God, you have truly blessed us. In a world of injustice, you promise to embrace us with your love. In the midst of our suffering, you promise us compassion. We know you love and care for the least among us. We confess we have not always shared your concern for them. Forgive us for our blindness toward the oppressed and teach us to care for them as we know you do. Prepare our hearts for the coming of Jesus. We pray in Advent hope. Amen.

## Day 23: Monday

## How do we serve Jesus?

Luke 1:26-33, 38

🔲 *Key Verse:* Then Mary said, "Here am I, the servant of the Lord; let it be with me according to your word." Then the angel departed from her. Luke 1:38

After the end of the Second World War, a Lutheran church member from Ohio responded to a call from God to go to New Guinea. The Japanese had retreated from the island protectorate, and the large Lutheran field was open, once again, for the arrival of missionaries.

This man was not theologically trained. But he had mechanical skills, and New Guinea needed men like him to build dams and hydroelectric plants on rushing mountain rivers. And so he went, at considerable risk. He had to relocate his entire family, taking them to the other side of the world. The journey included a two-month voyage on a steamship. There would be no furlough for five years. His parents, left behind, felt devastated. They were going to miss watching their grandchildren grow up. That realization gave him second thoughts about the decision to accept the assignment. He wondered whether he might not be dishonoring his parents, even as he obeyed God.

But he took the risk and followed his calling. Years later, many who came to know his work spoke in reverent admiration of what God had accomplished through him and his family in New Guinea.

Today's text tells the story of a frightened young woman with a seemingly impossible assignment. Mary knew that accepting God's calling for her would be risky. When she consented to being a vessel of the Holy Spirit, she changed the history of the world and enabled the salvation of humankind.

*Questions to Ponder*

· What might the result have been if Mary had said "no" to the angel Gabriel?
· When were you faced with a risky decision that seemed to be the only or best choice available to you at the time?

## Faith Connection

Mary's response to her unexpected and bewildering pregnancy has been set to music. For centuries Christians have sung "The Magnificat" (the name comes from the Latin word *to magnify*). This powerful hymn of praise appears in *Evangelical Lutheran Worship* as part of the service for evening prayer. Mary, Jesus' mother, showed in the words of this litany of praise her trust in God's purposes. She celebrates the trust that God has placed in her. Martin Luther was particularly impressed with Mary's response. He once said that Mary teaches us "with her words and by the example of her experience, how to know, love and praise God" (*Luther's Works*, Jaroslav Pelikan, ed., Concordia Publishing House, 1956, 21:301).

*Journal Reflections*

- What is your favorite hymn of praise, and why do you like it best?
- Where do you find the power to trust God when your head tells you to say no?

## The Work of Preparing

*We are Servants*

1.  Find the pictures (or photos) of yourselves that you added to your Advent tablecloth on Day 17.

2.  Beneath the whole group of figures, write "We are servants of the Lord," with each person using a different color and taking turns to write one letter at a time. (Or use letter stickers to spell out some or all of these words.)

3.  Optional (clean feet and adult supervision required): Make footprints under the words just added, as a reminder that God's servants are called to follow where God leads. Trace around each person's feet, or use paint on the bottom of your feet.

*Servants of the Lord*

1.  What words and thoughts come to mind when you hear the word "servant"?

2.  Reflect on some of these people and their calls to serve the Lord: Moses (Exodus 3:1—4:17), Joshua (Joshua 1:1-9), Samuel (1 Samuel 3:1-21), David (1 Samuel 16:1-13), and Mary (Luke 1:26-38). How does this affect your attitude toward the word "servant" and serving?

*Christmas Coupons*

1.  On index cards, write simple acts of service you will perform for friends or family members (tidying cupboards, doing the dishes, baking a cake, washing the car, etc.). State the frequency (once a week, for a month) and availability (on Saturday or Sunday mornings) of your gift. On the other side, write a Christmas greeting and sign your name.

2.  Give away your Christmas Coupons, and get ready to serve!

## Prayer for Today

Loving God, you call us to travel on unexpected roads, to destinations never seen before, in order to do for you that which sometimes seems beyond our ability to accomplish. Give us courage and wisdom to set out in faith, trusting your goodness the whole way through. Keep our eyes set on the one still to come. We pray in Advent hope. Amen.

*Day 24: Tuesday*

*How do we celebrate Jesus?*

Luke 1:39-45

*Key Verse:* As soon as I heard the sound of your greeting, the child in my womb leaped for joy. Luke 1:44

Several years ago the Lutheran Youth Organization in northwest Ohio held a gathering with the theme "Jesus is the light of my life." Attractive shirts were created for the event. Every participating teen was given one to wear. After the gathering, there were extra shirts. The organizers gave one to me, then a middle-aged man. It was my size, so I began to wear it.

Over the years, often when I'm out in public wearing my "Jesus shirt," strangers will stop me. One woman said, "I really love that shirt. And you obviously really love Jesus." It occurred to me that one way to celebrate the presence of Jesus in my life was to wear a message that allows me to share him with others. (I'm wearing the shirt as I write this.)

There are lots of ways to celebrate Jesus, some of them even more memorable than wearing his message on your shirt. Perhaps the most unusual of all was the response of John the Baptist. When he was still in his mother's womb, he gave a festive kick. It was as if he was trying to say, "If I was already born, I'd be jumping up and down for joy."

It's easy to get excited when we learn a loved one is going to give birth. It's even more imperative to celebrate an impending birth when the newborn will be successor to a throne. That was the situation with Mary's unborn child.

Jesus is coming soon. It's not too early to begin celebrating.

*Questions to Ponder*

- What parts of the Sunday worship service help you to celebrate Jesus in your life?
- What sort of jewelry or apparel do you wear that tells others that Jesus is the light of your life?

## Faith Connection

Some Christians regularly repeat the words spoken by Elizabeth in the Bible reading for today. They are included in a discipline called "the rosary." Lutherans have often avoided this practice, but Martin Luther followed it, because he had a high regard for Mary, the bearer of Christ. On one occasion, while Luther was taking refuge at Wartburg Castle, a fellow reformer took charge in Wittenberg, where Luther had been pastor and professor. The visiting pastor told people to get rid of their rosaries. When he returned, Luther declared that if the discipline helped nurture a Christian's devotional life, it should be allowed.

*Journal Reflections*

- Where do you experience Jesus' presence most readily in your daily life?
- How will you celebrate Jesus' presence in your home this week?

## The Work of Preparing

*Jesus Brings Joy*

1. Find the "Star of Christmas" you added to your Advent tablecloth on Day 22.
2. The coming of Jesus brings many things to the world, including joy. In the middle of your star, use letter stickers or different colors to spell out JESUS BRINGS JOY.
3. Optional: Around the star, add color, pictures, or stickers that remind you of the joy Jesus brings.

*Celebrating Jesus*

1. Flip through recent newspapers and magazines or search online for articles and advertisements for Christmas preparations and celebrations. What is the main focus of these?
2. Think about ways in which you can celebrate Jesus in your Christmas preparations and celebrations.

*Joyful Movement and Music*

1. Listen to some Christmas carols.
2. Improvise appropriate movements for the songs. Have fun with this.
3. Practice these movements together, then sing along and move to the music.

## Prayer for Today

Loving God, you give us much to celebrate. We are beneficiaries of every good thing that comes from your hand—life and health, good friends, favorable weather, leadership, and a hopeful future. We celebrate all that we have from you. Most of all, we give thanks that you have given us to Jesus and Jesus to us. Help us to welcome him fully into our lives. We pray in Advent hope. Amen.

*Day 25: Wednesday*

*How is God with us in Jesus?*

Matthew 1:18-25

🔲 *Key Verse:* "Look, the virgin shall conceive and bear a son, and they shall name him Emmanuel," which means, "God is with us." Matthew 1:23

Several years ago the Episcopal Church created a series of newspaper ads. They were aimed at people living on the edges of Christianity, including formerly active church members. A memorable ad in the series was one that pictured a chalice placed atop a television set. The caption read, "With all due respect, you can't take communion from a Sony."

The message was clear. Televised worship services are a poor substitute for meeting Jesus. Another way to put it would be this: We experience Jesus' presence most intimately when we share the sacrament of Holy Communion at public worship.

There are many ways we can experience God's presence in our lives. Lutherans have always believed that God is dramatically in our midst when Jesus meets us in bread and wine at the altar rail. Because of this belief, we do not treat this experience casually. We prepare ourselves.

Martin Luther once had a famous argument about Jesus' "real presence" at Holy Communion. It led to a centuries-long split between Lutherans and other Protestants. Luther's point was clear: when we receive the Sacrament, it's more than "sacred remembering." Jesus is really here.

In today's text the Gospel writer borrows a verse from the Old Testament, in order to give Jesus a powerful title. Emmanuel means "God with us." When we are in the presence of Jesus, we are in the presence of God. When we encounter him, we are actually encountering God.

*Questions to Ponder*

- What is your experience of Holy Communion? How do you feel after receiving the bread and the wine?
- Where do you meet Jesus beyond the doors of the church building?

## Faith Connection

The Gospel of Matthew often quotes from the Old Testament. In today's reading the quote comes from Isaiah 7:14. In its original context, the Emmanuel reference was to a child soon to be born in Israel as a sign to the king. (Isaiah's "Immanuel" and Matthew's "Emmanuel" are the same name.) Matthew has reinterpreted the Isaiah reference. When applied to Jesus, the story of a young woman soon to give birth takes on a new meaning. The readers of Matthew's Gospel likely knew the story from Isaiah. They also knew that, in a changed context, an old reference can tell a new story.

*Journal Reflections*

- How do you experience Jesus' presence when you are alone? How do you experience Jesus' presence with other believers?
- Why might a congregation choose "Emmanuel Lutheran" rather than "Christ Lutheran" for its name?

## The Work of Preparing

📖 *Jesus' Names are Wonderful!*

1. Write this heading on a blank area on your Advent tablecloth: "Jesus' names are wonderful!" (During the next few days, you will be adding to this list of names.)
2. Below the heading write (or use letter stickers to spell out), "Emmanuel—God is with us."
3. Next to the words just added, make a picture of the baby Jesus (with no straw, manger, and so on just yet). Leave some empty space around the baby.

📖 *God is with Us*

1. Set up or look at a nativity scene or picture, then reflect on how God is with us in Jesus.
2. Throughout the day, say to yourself, "Emmanuel—God is with us."

📖 *O Come, Emmanuel*

1. Sing the first verse of "O Come, Emmanuel." This song refers to a time when God's people were captives in Babylon. They prayed to God to come and "ransom" or save them. The birth of Jesus was an answer to that prayer. Jesus is called Emmanuel—God with us.
2. Sing "O Come, Emmanuel" again.

## Prayer for Today

Loving God, you have not abandoned us. Even though we do not encounter you in the flesh, we know you are with us. Help us to pattern our lives to give witness to you. Comfort us with your presence when we feel alone, and give us a sense of your purpose when we feel directionless. We pray in Advent hope. Amen.

## Day 26: Thursday

## What difference does it make that God chose to become human in Jesus?

John 1:14-18

> *Key Verse:* The Word became flesh and lived among us, and we have seen his glory, the glory as of a father's only son, full of grace and truth. John 1:14

Susan was two years old when her father went away to war. She had no memory of him. Her mother made every effort to tell her daughter about him. She showed Susan his photograph. She read portions of his letters to her whenever they arrived. She reminded her daughter, over and over, how much her father loved her. When she was four, Susan confronted her mother. "If Daddy loves me so much, why doesn't he ever come to see me?" Her mother's answer was, "He'll come when the war is over."

The war ended. Daddy came home. As Susan prepared herself to meet him, the reality of his coming set in. Much as she wanted him to come, she discovered she was frightened. Suppose she didn't really like him? Suppose he didn't really like her? When she finally saw him, her fears disappeared. He swept her up in a big hug. Later, when her mother asked her, "How do you like having Daddy here with us?," Susan replied, "I like it. You can't get a hug from pictures and letters."

John 1:14-18 is the story of God giving the entire world a hug. The people who waited for a coming Messiah always knew that God loved them. But the message had always come through messengers. With the arrival of Jesus in our world, everything changed. Suddenly we had a God in the flesh. Like a four-year-old child at a family reunion, God's people have their rescuer up close and personal. Things will never be the same again.

*Questions to Ponder*

- Does it diminish or enhance your view of God, knowing the Almighty became a human being?
- What difference would it have made if God had decided to remain majestically removed from our world?

## Faith Connection

Christians struggled for three centuries with a difficult question. Was God's Son truly human or did he only pretend to be? Some argued that God would lose his divinity by taking on human flesh. Others argued that our salvation depends on God having become truly human. After generations of debate, church leaders met in a series of gatherings to try to settle the issue of Jesus' divinity and humanity. While concluding that he was both human and divine, they declared this reality to be a paradox (two seemingly contradictory truths, both held in tension). The truth of Jesus' "two natures" remains a mystery. We may want to ask Jesus to explain it to us when we finally see him face to face.

*Journal Reflections*

- What do you think Jesus really looked like?
- Your hug is the passing along of God's cosmic embrace of us in Jesus. What do you think about this idea?

## The Work of Preparing

🔲 *Wonderful Word*

1. Locate the heading, "Jesus' names are wonderful" on your Advent table-cloth. Add this name to your list: "The Word."
2. Find the baby Jesus you added (Day 25). Cut or tear small strips of paper, and use glue to add this "straw" around the baby.

🔲 *The Word Became Flesh*

1. Think about the suffering and hardships human beings face. Jesus also experienced these things: hunger (Matthew 4:1-4), thirst (John 4:5-7, 19:28-30), agony (Mark 14:32-36), betrayal (Mark 14:43-50), rejection (Luke 4:24-30; John 6:60—7:5), loss and grief (Luke 11:32-36), ridicule (John 19:1-3; Mark 14:65, 15:16-32), abandonment (Mark 15:33-34), and death (Mark 15:37-39).
2. Despite the suffering and hardships, God *chose* to take on human flesh. How does that make you feel?

🔲 *Humans Created in God's Image*

1. This activity can be done with paper and markers or just through your imagination. Imagine you are the creator of all things. What changes would you make to human beings, knowing what you know now about our world? Have fun thinking about practical, but silly changes (tiny fingers for texting, built-in headphones for mp3 players). If you're drawing, be as free as you can.
2. Thank God for creating us the best way.

## Prayer for Today

Loving God, we celebrate your presence on earth through your Son. You have allowed us to know you, not only as a powerful ruler, but also as a friend and brother. When we endure times of pain and suffering, help us to remember that Jesus suffered in the flesh—for us. Prepare us for the day when we will see Jesus face to face. We pray in Advent hope. Amen.

## Day 27: Friday

## What does it mean that Jesus, God's Son, was born for us?

Isaiah 9:6-7

*Key Verse:* For a child has been born for us, a son given to us; authority rests upon his shoulders; and he is named Wonderful Counselor, Mighty God, Everlasting Father, Prince of Peace. Isaiah 9:6

Maude Grayling was quirky. Her husband, Elwin, had been the only one in his generation to carry on the family name. After he died, Maude had decided that the family home, a beautiful Victorian house on a hill, would only go to a male heir bearing the Grayling name. That eliminated her four daughters. Her son, Clarence, had no children. Maude had decided that, if a new generation of Graylings didn't appear, the wonderful old house, full of family memories, would be sold to strangers.

Therefore, when Clarence's wife Alice finally became pregnant, at age 43, a surge of hope swept through the family. But there was also trepidation. Alice had announced this would be her only child. What if the child was a girl? In due time Alice gave birth to Christopher, a healthy nine-pound baby boy. Maude was overjoyed. She willed her property to him. But the other members of the family were ecstatic. It was as if baby Christopher had been born for them. Because of his coming, their heritage was secure.

The people of Israel waited in hope for someone to come to their rescue. The prophet declared the arrival of a special newborn to be a moment of promise. When Jesus arrived in their midst, the first Christians remembered this amazing Bible text from Isaiah. It was obvious to them that the description fit Jesus. He brought with him hope for the future and blessings intended specifically for them. For more than two thousand years, Christians have celebrated Jesus' coming as a gift for them as well—the best gift anyone could have imagined.

### Questions to Ponder

- Since God intended Jesus as a gift for the entire world, why is it that some people don't receive him in that way?
- What gives you assurance that Jesus' coming was also for you and not only for other people?

## Faith Connection

It's not uncommon, when attending a celebration where gifts are presented, to hear a familiar response: "For me? You shouldn't have." What is really intended by this comment? One possibility is that the recipient isn't sure he or she actually deserves it. Martin Luther reminds us that God provides for us in a way that we do not deserve. In his explanation to Article 1 of the Apostles' Creed, Luther says that every child of God receives everything out of "divine goodness and mercy, without any merit or worthiness of mine at all!" (*Luther's Small Catechism with* Evangelical Lutheran Worship *Texts*, gift edition, Timothy J. Wengert, trans., Augsburg Fortress, 2008, p. 13). Chief among God's gifts, intended for each of us as beloved children, is Jesus himself.

*Journal Reflections*

- What can you do to practice accepting a gift more gracefully?
- How will you thank God for the gift to you of Jesus?

## The Work of Preparing

🗨 *More Marvelous Names*

1.  Add these names to the list of Jesus' names on your Advent tablecloth: "Wonderful Counselor," "Mighty God," "Everlasting Father," "Prince of Peace."

2.  Jesus is God's gift to us and the world. Just below the baby Jesus and straw you added (Days 25 and 26), draw a box or manger. (Or take a separate piece of paper, cut out a rectangle, and glue it under the baby and straw.)

🗨 *What's in a Name?*

1.  In Bible times, a name was not merely an identification tag. A name represented a person's character, and calling on that name invoked that person's power. Meditate for a few minutes on each of the four names mentioned in today's Bible passage: Wonderful Counselor, Mighty God, Everlasting Father, Prince of Peace. What do each of these names suggest about God and Jesus?

🗨 *Praise His Names*

1.  Gather together near a nativity scene, Christmas lights, or a Christmas tree.

2.  Sing songs which praise the wonderful names of Jesus ("Jesus Loves Me," "Away in a Manger," "Praise the Name of Jesus," "His Name Is Wonderful," "His Name is Higher," "Jesus, Name above All Names").

## Prayer for Today

Loving God, you give us everything we need. Like children who cannot survive without a caring parent, we depend on you for life and health and every good thing. We are overwhelmed with the gift you made to us through your Son, whose life and death and resurrection assure us a place in your everlasting kingdom. Keep us looking toward the future you have prepared for us. We pray in Advent hope. Amen.

## Day 28: Saturday

## What will we do with this good news about Jesus?

Luke 2:8-20

*Key Verse:* To you is born this day in the city of David a Savior, who is the Messiah, the Lord. Luke 2:11

When the Allied Armies marched into Germany in the spring of 1945, they discovered the concentration camps created by the Third Reich. While the liberators had come too late for some, there were many prisoners still waiting to be released. In many of the camps, when the gates were opened and the survivors were told they were free to go, they didn't believe what they were hearing. Some of them held back, not sure whether it was safe to leave or not. Others took the liberating forces at their word and walked to freedom.

The Gospel writer tells the story of shepherds taking care of their flocks in the middle of the night. Suddenly they were hearing unbelievable news, coming from the heavens. It all seemed astonishing—too good to be true. They may have thought they were hallucinating. Imagine the conversation they might have had among themselves after the angels disappeared. It might have gone like this:

"Did you hear what I heard?" "Were they making that up?" "Were *we* making it up?" "Why would good news like that come to hired hands like us?" "Can we believe it?" "I don't know. Maybe we should go and find out."

What do you do when you hear unbelievably good news? The best thing to do is to take it seriously, and see where it leads you. When the news is that God has come to be with us in person, who can guess where that might lead?

*Questions to Ponder*

- When, if ever, have you received a valuable gift that you never really used?
- Since something "too good to be true" usually isn't, why should we believe such news about Jesus?

## Faith Connection

Of the four Gospels in the New Testament, only Luke tells us about angels appearing to shepherds. One possible reason is that only Luke knew the story. It sometimes happens when research is done, prior to the writing of a biography of a notable person, that only one individual knows a given piece of information. Without that individual's report, a key to understanding the notable person would be lost. Not everyone knows the real importance of Jesus as the center of human history. Those who do know have an opportunity, and a responsibility, to speak up at appropriate times and in appropriate ways.

*Journal Reflections*

- When have you held back from telling something you knew when it could have been of help to others?
- Is a report more or less credible when it comes from an ordinary person—such as a shepherd, or a theologically untrained follower of Jesus? Why do you think so?

## The Work of Preparing

*Good News of Great Joy*

1.  Return to your list of Jesus' names on the Advent tablecloth, and add "Savior," "Messiah," "Lord."
2.  Invite a family member, neighbor, or friend to your home to see your Advent tablecloth and share a meal or snack with you.

*Sharing the Good News*

1.  Consider the sequence of events in today's Bible passage. The shepherds heard the good news about the Messiah (Luke 2:8-14). They saw the Messiah for themselves (Luke 2:15-16). They shared what they had seen and heard with others (Luke 2:17-18). They praised God for this great news (Luke 2:20).
2.  How will you share the good news of Jesus?

*Let's Sing!*

Sing the following words to the tune of "Jingle Bells." Add instruments and actions if you wish. (Note: Jesus was born in Bethlehem, which means "house of bread" in Hebrew, and Bread of Life is another name for Jesus.)

Refrain:

Clap and sing, clap and sing, sing a joyful song

When we have good news to share, we're happy all day long, oh

Clap and sing, clap and sing, joyful news we bring

Like the angels long ago,

Let's sing, let's sing, let's sing

Verse:

In the House of Bread, the Bread of Life is born

Jesus is his name, Bethlehem's the town

Angel hosts on high, singing songs of praise

Glory to our God, they cry, and so sing you and I, oh

## Prayer for Today

Loving God, we have been loved into your everlasting family by the arrival in our world of your powerful Son. Teach us to love as you do, and to tell everyone we know about Jesus. In his powerful name we pray. Amen.